MW00778737

# GOD SPEAKS
# HEARING GOD'S VOICE IN YOUR LIFE

By

Dr. Danny Lee Brooks

Published by GodisforYou,

Haleyville, Alabama
Copyright 2018

# ACKNOWLEDGEMENTS

I originally wrote this book for my thesis while getting my doctorate. I let several family members and friends read it after I submitted it to school, and they subsequently encouraged me that I should eventually get it published. After prayer about the matter, I realized that what I had learned in my life about listening and hearing God's voice could help others.

As such, I would like to thank my wonderful parents, Ruby and Billy Brooks, my brother, Phillip Brooks, my sister Margaret Capelton, and my daughters, Andrea, and Kristen for their words of love, encouragement, and support. I would also like to thank my editor, Susan Allen, for her editing, as well as her theological input into the book. Susan is a RHEMA Bible College graduate. I also want to acknowledge Mary Moore, who helped us greatly with proofreading and editing. Special thanks to Amy Brown for her help with the cover design and layout and to Pastor Benny Knight, of Solid Rock Church, Haleyville, Alabama.

# TABLE Of CONTENTS

# Chapter 1
## God's Miracle for Margaret

The doctor told Margaret's parents, "Take your baby home. If she is still alive in two weeks, bring her back." That was a sad report from a doctor, but that was the report given to Billy and Ruby Brooks on an autumn day of 1957. This was after they had been asked to sign papers that would allow the doctors to perform an autopsy on their baby. That permission was not granted. Ruby replied, "My baby is not dead, and I will not sign your papers."

After leaving the hospital, Billy, Ruby, and baby Margaret, went to the home of Ruby's parents, Velmon and Rosie Shirley. Their house was filled with love and the abiding presence of God.

Velmon was a man who deeply loved God, his family, and friends. Velmon had little formal education. He was a coal miner, but he had a heart that knew how to reach the throne of God. He knew very well his Lord and Master. Velmon walked in a close relationship with the "Good Lord". It was a phrase he used often. Rosie was a Proverbs 31 lady.

Billy and Ruby told Velmon and Rosie, what the doctor had said about baby Margaret. Velmon replied, "That may be what the doctor said, but the doctor does not have the last word! We are going to pray to the Good Lord for Margaret's life, health, and healing." That's exactly what they did. God heard and answered their prayers! God also answered by sending wisdom to Billy, Margaret's dad.

Margaret had been in the hospital for several weeks. She was born with many health issues that required surgery. The doctors had removed most of her intestines. She was unable to keep milk on her stomach. Margaret was living on glucose that was being given to her through her veins. The doctors at Children's Hospital reasoned that if she could not keep milk on her stomach, she would not live outside of the hospital for very long.

In James 1:5, God's word says, *"If any of you lacks wisdom, let him ask of God, who gives to all liberally and without reproach, and it will be given to him."*

Jesus healed in many different types of ways when He walked among men. God is Good and very diverse. Some try to limit Him to doing things only one way. This can be a mistake. I have truly learned that He is The Way, The Truth, and The Life.

In Mark 8:23, Jesus led a blind man out of town, and strangely spit on the man's eyes. As Jesus put His hands on him, He asked if he saw anything. The man said, "I see men like trees walking." Jesus then put His hands on the man again and made him look up. The blind man believed, obeyed, and was healed! He saw everyone clearly!

I know some of you will say, yes, but that was Jesus, and He could do anything. Let's look a little deeper. In John 5:19, Jesus says, *"The Son can do nothing of Himself, but what He sees the Father do; for whatever He does, the Son also does in like manner."* Jesus came to earth as a man! He came wrapped in the skin of a baby! He was one hundred percent God. Jesus was God's only begotten Son, but He came here as a man. So, how did He perform these marvelous works and healings, and speak with such profound inspiration and authority?  He was very sensitive to the leadership of the Spirit of God.  He started His ministry by fasting and prayer.  As Jesus was baptized by John, the Holy Spirit fell on Him in the form of a dove.  Then God spoke from heaven and said, "This is my beloved Son, in whom I am well pleased."

It was then that He went into the wilderness, where He fasted and prayed for forty days and forty nights.  Jesus was victorious over the devil by quoting the Word of God.  He was living through the Word and the Spirit of God!   He was 100% man but was totally sold out to God!  Yes, He was and is God, but He came here as man.  He did not do His own bidding but did only what the Father spoke and showed Him to do.   Now that is wisdom!  Since Jesus needed this kind of direction while here on earth, how about us?   Is that not the ultimate pinnacle of wisdom for all of us?  The answer is yes, being led of God's Spirit is the ultimate pinnacle of wisdom.

God answered the prayers of Margaret's parents, and grandparents, by sending wisdom to Billy, Margaret's father.  He said, "Let's give her one ounce of milk each hour.  She may cry for more, but we know she cannot keep any more on her stomach."   The wisdom of God, through the Spirit of God said, "Only one ounce."  In obedience to the Lord, they all acted on this and then waited with great faith.

Praise God!  Margaret was able to keep the milk on her stomach, one ounce at a time!   This required a lot of patience, and love, to only give her a bottle once an hour around the clock.  They

had to listen to her cry for more, but "she lived!"
Praise God!   God is faithful!

In two weeks, Margaret was taken back to
Children's Hospital in Birmingham, Alabama.  The
doctor was amazed to see that she was still alive!
He wanted to know why she was still alive.  The
doctor asked, "What did you do?  Others could
benefit from knowing this information."  The nurses
took Margaret in their arms and paraded her up
and down the halls!  The other doctors in the
hospital were all informed as to why Margaret was
still alive.

Margaret grew up and got married.  She was told to
never get pregnant. The doctors believed that she
was unable to nourish a baby.  Her food did not stay
inside of her long enough to digest properly.  But
God!!!  Her digestive system worked well enough
and she did become pregnant.  She gave birth to a
fine, baby boy, named Branden Lee Capelton!   The
miracle girl Margaret, had a miracle baby boy named
Branden!   Praise God!  He is faithful!

The doctors were convinced that it was
impossible for Margaret to have a child.  However,
Jesus taught us in Matthew 19:26, that things
which seem impossible to men are possible to
God!  We can trust Him!  He sees the future.   He
knows what is ahead.   No detail escapes Him.
When we have done all that we know to do
according to God's Word, and praying the prayer
of faith, we must simply trust and wait on God.   He
will not fail us, no not ever!

Yes, God is amazing!  He loves us!  He speaks to
us!  It's up to us to be still and hear His voice. The
Bible tells us in 1 Corinthians 1:21, *"Eye has not
seen, nor ear heard, nor have entered into the*

*heart of man the things which God has prepared for those who love Him."* Now I realize that text has been used at many funerals. However, it is referring to God speaking to our spirit, and the things He has in mind for us here and now. The text goes on to say in the next verse, *"But God has revealed them to us through His Spirit. For the Spirit searches all things, yes, the deep things of God."* By accepting Jesus, as our Savior and Lord of our life, then we can walk with the mind of Christ. He tells us this in 1 Corinthians 2:16, *"For who has known the mind of the Lord that he may instruct him? But we have the mind of Christ."*

Does the Holy Spirit of God know all things? The answer, of course, is yes! Then why would we not ask Him about everything?

Margaret, the miracle baby, is my only sister! My Mom and Dad had a child born two years later, Phillip, and then two years later, I was born.

I am thankful for a good Christian brother. My brother Phillip loves the Lord. He attends a church called Grace House, in Florence, Alabama. He gets excited listening to his Pastor, Dr. Eddie Lawrence, proclaim God's Word in Spirit and truth. I admire Phillip for his wisdom, integrity, and character. If I need advice or help, he is always there.

I must say that I am a very blessed person to have been raised in a Christian home! Praise God! I'm sure I speak for my brother and sister in saying that we all were blessed in our upbringing. (I do realize that not everyone has been raised in a Christian home, or even had good parents.) Praise God, when we have Jesus in our hearts

God becomes our Father!

He teaches us in His Word in Galatians 4:6-7, *"....and because you are sons, God has sent forth the Spirit of His Son into your hearts, crying out, Abba, Father! Therefore, you are no longer a slave but a son, and if a son then an heir of God through Christ."* We are sons and daughters of God, through salvation in Christ Jesus. I recently heard a message by a local pastor. He said that if Satan can affect or disrupt the relationship with your natural father, he can achieve the goal of making you distrust God as your heavenly father. Our natural father is to be a type and shadow of God, our heavenly father. If you have been blessed, like I have been blessed to have a wonderful dad, you are able to trust God more fully and be more confident in His amazing love. When you have had a dysfunctional relationship with your father, it is difficult to understand the heights and depths of God's love for you. You might view God as unapproachable, distant, and hard. However, that is simply not true!!! God is a good God! He is good all the time! His thoughts towards you are good!!! Right now, take a moment and ask God to give you a revelation of His true nature. He is a kind, merciful, and a loving God, who wants nothing more than for you to know how much He loves you and wants the best for you. Run to Him, and let Him be your daddy, your "Abba father."

# Chapter 2
## Prayers Answered in Mississippi

Luke 18:16 says, ***"But Jesus called them to Him and said, Let the little children come to me, and do not forbid them; for of such is the kingdom of God."*** Jesus hears and answers the prayers of children. He has a heart for them.

I can remember, as a four-year old child, living in Mississippi, when my mother was very sick. She was in a small-town hospital. The treatment she received there was not very good. She had a severe kidney infection. She was so sick, that my father was told to take her by car to a bigger hospital in Hattiesburg. The infection was so bad, that there was no time to wait for an ambulance.

Upon arrival at the Hattiesburg hospital, my mom was seen by a doctor who cursed profusely. She had lost thirty pounds in seven days. He was upset because the doctor at the smaller hospital, had allowed her to get in such bad condition. Mom got up to leave. The nurse said, "Where are you going?"

My mom told her that she could not take anyone using God's name in vain. The doctor decided to stop cussing in front of her, and so she stayed. Mom's life was in great jeopardy. It appeared she had only hours to live.

My mom prayed to live. She heard this in her Spirit, "The answer is on the way." That answer came in the form of prayer warriors! Her Mom, Dad, their Pastor, and friends, came from Alabama, and they prayed!

I can remember that I prayed, "God, I'm just a little boy. I need my Mom, please let her live, at least until I get grown."

God heard all those prayers many years ago, and she is still with us! Today my mom is in her seventies, still worshipping God, and cooks and cleans.

Later, that same doctor said that the small-town doctor had sent my mom to him, to pull her back from the grave. However, I know it was the hand of God guiding and healing, that performed the miracle! Let me tell you, "Prayer changes people!" God uses prayer to change sick people into healed people!

God says in Mark 16:18, referring to born again Christians, that they shall lay hands on the sick, and they shall recover!

Another interesting prayer that was answered in Mississippi, was prayed by the neighbor, Mrs. Sam Graham who lived across the street. They told my mom that they were related to Dr. Billy Graham. They belonged to a local Full Gospel Church. Mrs. Graham was very nice to me and wanted me to come and eat her homemade dumplings! I thought they tasted wonderful! Isn't it interesting the things you remember from your early childhood?

The Graham's church believed that if you did not have the gift of tongues, or the baptism of the Holy Spirit, you were not saved. Sister Graham did not believe that, but still earnestly wanted the gift of speaking in tongues. She had decided she would not settle for anything but the real thing. She made a covenant with God. She met with God every day under an apple tree. Sister Graham prayed for the Spirit of God to manifest the gift of tongues through her, and after six months she received the gift of tongues. She also received Holy Laughter! She would get happy in the Spirit of God! The joy of the Lord is our strength!

Sister Graham's grandson invited her to go to the Methodist Church Revival. She warned him that she might get carried away in the Spirit. He wanted her to come anyway. They sat on the back bench. That preacher started preaching, and she said the next thing she knew she was lost in the Spirit, praying in tongues, and Holy laughter! She said when she came to herself, the preacher looked at her and said, "Now that's the kind of religion my grandmother had." The service broke loose after that! God's Spirit was mighty in the service! I have often wondered if part of Dr. Billy Graham's ministry success was due to a praying, Spirit filled relative!

I know it is God's will to give the gift of the Spirit of God to His children! You don't need to seek this wonderful gift for six months before receiving it!! Don't you know His presence was so special to Sister Graham after all that time she spent seeking Him? God honored her time spent in prayer, and worship, by giving her a sweet gift of His Spirit. She was filled with His presence, love, laughter, and tongues!

Luke 11:9-13, *"So I say to you, ask, and it will be given to you; seek, and you will find; knock, and it will be opened to you. For everyone who asks receives, and he who seeks finds, and to him who knocks it will be opened. If a son asks for bread from any father among you, will he give him a stone? Or if he asks for a fish, will he give him a serpent instead of a fish? Or if he asks for an egg, will he offer him a scorpion? If you then, being evil, know how to give good gifts to your children, how much more will your heavenly Father give the Holy Spirit to those who ask Him?"*

I encourage you today to seek the Lord and ask Him to reveal to you, by His Word, the truth concerning His spiritual gifts, and the complete work of the infilling of the Holy Spirit. I believe it will bring you into a deeper, more intimate relationship with your Heavenly Father than you could ever imagine. I hope you will see and receive revelation knowledge the further you read in this book about all that God has for you. I believe this book will help you discover the amazing benefits of all of His spiritual gifts.

# Chapter 3
## Salvation

In John 3:3, Jesus said, *"Most assuredly, I say to you, unless one is born again, he cannot see the kingdom of God."* Jesus continued in verse 16 to say, *"For God so loved the world that He gave His only begotten son, that whosoever believes in Him should not perish but have everlasting life."* There is nothing an individual can do in this life that is as important as giving their heart to Jesus Christ! It's is the most important decision you will ever make in your life.

I remember how, as a thirteen-year old boy, I was sitting in a country church during a revival. The Spirit of God convicted me of my sin, and I went forward, and asked God to forgive me. I invited Jesus to come into my heart and be my Lord and Savior. Praise God, He did! I wish I could say that I walked a closer walk with God without ever looking back but I can't. After a few years, I began to be influenced by those I was hanging around, and I started living for myself. That kind of decision only brings trouble and lack of peace. A few years later, I ran into some people in a cafe that I went to church with when I was growing up. They invited me to come to church. The name of that church is Beech Grove Baptist Church. One of the individuals in that group was Frank Holder. He was teaching Sunday school.

Now, even though I was not going to church, I was raised to believe a person should keep their word. I knew I would be going to a service at Beech Grove soon. When I did, Brother Frank was teaching out of the book of Job. He read where

God spoke to Job out of the whirlwind.  Job 38:4-6 says, *"Where were you when I laid the foundations of the earth?  Tell me, if you have understanding.  Who determined its measurements?  Surely you know!  Or who stretched the line upon it? To what were its foundations fastened?  Or who laid its cornerstone?"*

I thought about that passage asking myself, "Where was I?"  I saw myself as so small compared to a big and wise God.  What was life without Him?

God had been dealing with me through different people and events.  I remember calling my grandparents, Velmon and Rosie Shirley.  They told me they were praying for me every day.  I hung up the phone and wept thinking of God's love, and their love for me.  Thank God for a praying family!  While my family was busy praying for me, God was also using other people in my life to reach out to me.  They would help me find my way back to my heavenly father.  I had some customers in Lumberton, North Carolina named The Scott Sisters.  These precious ladies had a floral shop that I called on for my business.  They had a gospel singing group as well.  I had gotten some of their music, and I would ride and listen to it.

One day, as I was going to the Scott Sisters' shop, I stopped at a fast food place to get a hamburger.  A man came up to me and asked if I would buy him some food.  I told him I would be happy to buy him a meal, and for him to go ahead and order it, and I would pay for it.  He ordered one hamburger and a drink.  I thought it odd that he did not order more. He then asked me to sit with him. As we talked, and ate our meal, that man was saying things to me that were so uplifting! Here I was feeling so down about myself, because I knew that I needed a closer relationship with the Lord. This man was seeing something good in me! He was encouraging me in the Lord! It was powerful! I've often wondered since then if he was a man, or an angel sent from God. Hebrews 13:2 says, *"Do not forget to entertain strangers, for by so doing some have unwittingly entertained angels."*

A few days later, I was going through the Bankhead Forest in my one-ton truck, pulling a thirty-six-foot trailer. I was listening to The Scott Sisters. As they sang, the Spirit of God was drawing me unto Himself. I cried out to God and asked Him to forgive me of my sins. He did, and a great burden was lifted from my heart. God is full of love and compassion!

Before I cried out to God that day, I had a lot of hate in my heart for a man that had previously worked for me. He had stolen about $10,000 worth of my company's merchandise. Honestly, I wanted to get even with him. However, God brought him up before my face. God revealed to me that I must forgive this man and let go of what he had done to me. I told God, "I forgive that man." Then I prayed for him. A few days after I had prayed for him, I went to have my car serviced. He was there working, and I started speaking to him. I believe he was probably thinking we were about to fight when he saw me. He was shaking. I told him that I knew what he had done. He said he would pay everything he had stolen back. I told him he did not have to do that, but he had better get his heart right with God. I knew I had every right to prosecute this man for what he had done, but I chose not to pursue any action against him. Unfortunately, this man plunged deeper into sin. He is now in the penitentiary for the rest of his life for crimes he committed later. God tried to warn him, but he would not listen.

After rededicating my heart to the Lord, my life has been interesting and so good! God has spoken into my spirit in many ways and at various times.

I am so glad God loves us, and He desires for us to be with Him forever! It is very sad that some people say God is not even real. The Bible says in Psalm 14:1, *"The fool has said in his heart, there is no God."*

My mother told me once that not believing in God is like a person walking through the woods, hungry and cold. They come upon a house with smoke coming out of the chimney. They knock, but no one answers the door. They go inside and smell the food that is cooking on the stove. They decide in their mind that no one has been there. Somehow, they conclude that the house and food just appeared, or happened to be there. When we hear that, we could easily say that surely no person could come to such an illogical conclusion. Honestly, it's easier to believe that story than it is to believe that a complex world, and universe, just appeared! God made this universe and us! He loves us, knows us, and speaks to us! Are we listening?

Adam and Eve walked with God and knew Him intimately! He was their closest friend! They could have enjoyed this fellowship forever, but they listened to the serpent and ate of the forbidden fruit. Afterward, they hid. God asked why, and they said it was because they were naked. God asked them, in Genesis 3:11, ***"Who told you that you were naked? Have you eaten from the tree of which I commanded you that you should not eat?"*** Adam blamed Eve, and Eve blamed the serpent.

But why did Adam even realize that he was naked? Maybe it was because sin had entered in, and his innocence was gone. Just like a little baby can laugh and feel no shame about being naked, Adam and Eve had known that kind of innocence. It was gone, and sin had taken its place.

God covered them with tunics of animal skin and turned them out of The Garden of Eden. When an animal is skinned, there is shedding of blood. That animal skin covering points us to the Lamb of God, the Lord Jesus Christ. God sent His Only Begotten Son, who would shed His blood so that our relationship with the Father could be restored! Praise God for Jesus!

The blood of Adam flows through all of us, and we have something inside of us that longs for that intimacy that man once enjoyed with our Father God!

There is a void that longs to be filled. Men and women try to fill that void with money, fame, power, lust, and many other things, but it just does not work. That void can only be filled by God, and there is only one way to God. Every sacrifice in the Old Testament pointed to the One who would come and shed His blood, for the sins of the world!

God chose to become one of us by sending His

Son into the world, born of a virgin named Mary. His Son was Jesus, and His Father is God. Jesus is God's Son. He came into to this world as a man. He lived a life without sin. He did nothing of Himself but only did what the Father told him! Jesus said in John 5:22, ***"I can of Myself do nothing, As I hear I judge; and my judgement is righteous, because I do not seek My own will but the will of the Father who sent me."***

God is in the business of restoring unity. The unity that existed in the Garden of Eden before the fall was very special! The price to restore that unity came at a great cost. Jesus hung on a cross as the ultimate sacrifice for your sin and for mine. The Old Testament points to Him throughout its pages. From man's fall to that moment on the cross, Jesus was the bridge to restore the unity between God and man.

Something happened on that cross that I believe we cannot fully comprehend this side of heaven. Jesus had always been with God the Father and had walked in perfect unity with Him on this earth. He had never been alone because the Father was always with Him. The Bible tells of a strange thing happening in Mark 15:34, ***"And at the ninth hour Jesus cried out with a loud voice, saying, Eloi Eloi, lama sabachthani? which is translated, My God, My God, why have You forsaken me?"*** Could it be that Jesus could not die hanging there as God? Did God remove His Spirit from Jesus, as the sin of the world was put on Him? If so, then we can surely understand in part His crying out about being forsaken. He had never been alone. Suddenly, He was alone, and had all the sin of the world for all time put upon Him. Surely Jesus has a special love for us to pay such a high price!

I am so glad we serve a God full of love and mercy! I am proud to know that I am saved, and my sins are forgiven. I am glad that my name is written in the Lamb's Book of Life! I will never be alone, because Jesus was willing to pay the high cost for your soul and for mine!

I am so thankful that God speaks to us as His creation. One of the most important ways that He speaks is by that inward tug at a person's heart. Many unbelievers have had that experience as He calls one to salvation. After salvation, He speaks often in that still, small voice into our spirits. A person may have had many people in their life to speak to them, including parents, siblings, school acquaintances, coworkers, and even strangers on the streets. Yet no one person, or a person's voice, is as important as that still, small voice that tugs inwardly from God. It's as if He is saying, "I love you, and I have created you for a relationship with me! Turn your back on sin and accept the price that my Son paid on the cross to restore our relationship!"

We did not go searching for God, but He came searching for us. In John 15:16, Jesus said that we did not choose Him, but that He chose us. Each one of us is of great value to God!

# Chapter 4
## Godly Friends

After I got saved, events began happening that would forever change my life. I was selling artificial flowers and floral supplies off my truck in South Georgia. I had a customer there whose name was Sister Faye. She is a mighty lady of God! I was in her shop, and one of her customers was talking about being healed in a service at the fellowship where Sister Faye attended. Her customer said she had a goiter on her neck. The Pastor had prayed in Jesus' name, and it came off! Praise God! There were other miracles happening as well. A man who had been in that service had stomach cancer. After the service, as he was headed home, he pulled over and threw up. Everyone knows there is nothing pleasant, or good looking about vomit, but what came out was green. He was healed of cancer! Praise God! There are benefits to serving Him!

Sister Faye wanted me to meet her pastor. His name was Brother Glenn Taylor. She had given me a CD of his testimony to listen to. It was wonderful! God had done such a great work in this precious man's life. Brother Glenn went to be with Jesus in 2010, at the age of 64. He had led an exciting life. I would like to share some of his amazing testimony with you here.

When Glenn Taylor was young, he had a great desire to get rich. He got into the tractor and farm equipment business. When he was still in his twenties, he became a wealthy man. He had a nice home, many vehicles, and an airplane. He was a very successful man by the world's standards. He had a pretty wife as well. He thought he had accomplished everything he needed to be happy. Yet, there was still something missing in his life. Brother Glenn said what was missing was peace. He had a lot of money, and things, but no peace.

Brother Glenn told how he attended a convention at a resort on a tropical island. He had won a silver cup for selling more equipment than anyone in his region. It appeared that he was at the pinnacle of his career, but in reality, his life was in chaos. Brother Glenn had gotten hooked on drugs, needing pills in the mornings that would keep him "up". He would have to take "downers" mixed with whiskey at night to go to sleep. The day he received that award, he threw that silver cup that he had won on the bed. He was totally disgusted because something was missing from his life. All that money and recognition meant nothing, because he did not have peace.

Brother Glenn shared how he got himself locked into the commodities market buying commodity future contracts. If the contracts went up, he made a lot of money. If the contracts went down, he lost money and could continue to lose even more. He continued to trade in these contract futures, and eventually made a lot of money. This kind of trading had considerable risks, and he got hooked into one of those deals that he could not get out of. Brother Glenn lost a tremendous amount of money, until finally the commodities market broke him.

Brother Glenn told of his wife leaving him, and how he decided to commit suicide. He was going down the road in a new pickup truck. He passed a car and intended to run off a bridge and end it all. He said he was thinking about how bad his wife would feel for being the reason he had killed himself. It's amazing the lies demonic spirits will speak to a person if they will listen.

Brother Glenn's mother was hanging out clothes on the clothes line when God spoke to her and said, "Pray for Glenn. He is in trouble." She prayed, and a wheel came off his truck! He hit the bridge but did not die! He totaled the pickup but only got a cut on his chin. He had that scar as long as he lived. There is power in a praying mother!

It seems that things get done in this life because someone is praying or following what God told them to do in prayer. We are God's hands and feet on this earth. Some want angels to intervene on their behalf or that of others. According to the Word of God, all we must do is to ask!

Brother Glenn told about how he went on to get established in another business. His first wife never came back, and they got divorced. He then married a lady named Nancy. They were married for many years, until he died.

This new business was prosperous for a season but soon began to experience money problems. He had written out $200,000 worth of checks that people were holding. Brother Glenn was going to have an auction to raise the money to cover the checks. Unfortunately, the IRS came to the auction and took the money. Brother Glenn panicked, got his children, and left the state. Now he was wanted for kidnapping his own children because he left the state without telling their mother. He had intentions of leaving the United

States and going to South America. His plan was that he would fly airplanes for hire. Before he could do that, he was arrested and taken to jail.

While in jail he said to God, "Why did you do this to me?" Then God spoke to Brother Glenn and said to him, "I did not do this to you. You did it to yourself."

Brother Glenn finally cried out to God. He asked God to save him and fill him with His Spirit! God did, and he began to see supernatural things happen in his life. He led several men to Christ.

His aunt came to visit him in jail, and he told her he was coming home for Thanksgiving. She went and told his wife, Nancy, that Glenn was losing his mind. She told Nancy what he had said. Nancy questioned her a bit further. Glenn told his aunt how God had spoken that into his spirit. Nancy said, "I had better start cooking!" The aunt said, "You have both lost your minds!"

God told Brother Glenn to tell his cell mates that he was going home for Thanksgiving. He did. They said, "That is great, bring us some cookies back!" They did not believe him. They had a big laugh.

On Thanksgiving morning, Brother Glenn was in the jailhouse yard sweeping. The sheriff saw him and told him to go put on some street clothes. The sheriff had to go to another county to carry some paperwork and wanted Glenn to ride along. Brother Glenn was excited to go.

On the way back, the sheriff looked at Brother Glenn and told him he was going to do him a favor. He had decided to let Nancy meet them in town. He even told Glenn he could give Nancy a kiss. About that time, the sheriff spotted a car on the side of the road that was broken down with no driver. He asked Brother Glenn if that was his car. He said, "Yes." The sheriff then asked him, "So how is Nancy going to get out here to see you? Maybe we should call her." Brother Glenn said, "She does not have a phone." The sheriff said, "I don't know why I am doing this, but I'm going to carry you out to your house and let you see Nancy." When they got out there, the sheriff replied, "Just look at all the cars. Why, you would have thought they were expecting you!" Nancy had just come outside and overheard the Sheriff say that. She told him that they were expecting him. They went in and ate. Brother Glenn's mother was there. She looked at Brother Glenn and said, "Son, I am so proud of you!" He said, "What do you mean Mother? I've been rich, but now I'm broke and in jail." She said, "I know son, but now you have got Jesus in your heart. I held you up before God when you were a baby. I said God make a preacher out of him.'"

As they were walking out the door, Nancy asked if she could give Glenn cookies to carry with him. The sheriff said he could only take them if he shared them with the other guys. Brother Glenn said he would not have had it any other way! He said when they got back, he did not say anything, but just laid the cookies down in front of the guys! He let them ask the questions!

Brother Glenn's case was about to go to trial, and he was laughing, when his lawyer said, "Son, you have nothing to laugh about." The lawyer was cursing as he said, "You are looking at many years in the penitentiary." Brother Glenn told the lawyer if that was the way he felt, he was fired! The lawyer asked him who was going to represent him. He said he would go without a lawyer and depend on the Holy Ghost! The lawyer told him he did not have a "snowball's chance in hell"!

Brother Glenn went into the courtroom trusting God, and got three years, of which he served half. When he had entered the penitentiary, and the door shut behind him, he heard God say, "Welcome to Bible College son. You would not listen and do it the way I wanted you to. In here, you will learn to discern every evil spirit."

They asked him in the penitentiary what he wanted to do as far as work. Brother Glenn said he wanted to work in the chaplain department. They told him he had just arrived, and it was not happening.

Later he went to lunch. He asked God where to sit. God directed him where to sit. He bowed his head and prayed over his food. A man at the other end of the table asked his name. Then the man asked Brother Glenn what he had received as a job assignment at the penitentiary. He told him he had just arrived and had no job. The man said, "I work for the chaplain department. I will see that you get my job. I am leaving." He did, in fact, get the job!

He reported to work the next day. They put him to cleaning floors. God spoke to him and told him to take the valances down on a long hall and wash them. He did. An officer came by and bragged on that. He asked Brother Glenn who told him to do that. He replied, "God!" They sent him to the prison psychiatrist! He led the psychiatrist to Jesus! Praise God!

After Brother Glenn got out of the penitentiary, he

preached tent revivals for eighteen years.

While he was doing the work of an evangelist, a lady gave him a prophecy. It was at a meeting in Missouri. She told him that God was going to relocate him a certain number of miles away. I think it was 583 miles. I do not remember the precise number. She told him the place would be southeast from where they were standing. She went on to say that there would be a white house, cows, and water.

A few years later, Brother Glenn was filling in for a church without a pastor. The name of that church is Covenant Christian Church, in Douglas, Georgia. He brought in several preachers to minister to them while he was there. After a while, he met with the elders, and asked which minister they had chosen. They said they had prayed, and all felt that he was the man for the job. He told them that he was an evangelist and not a pastor. They asked him if he would at least pray about it. He said he would.

When he prayed about becoming their pastor, he was at the church. God said, "Walk outside son." When he did, he saw a white house, cows, and a pond. He went and looked at a map. The prophecy the lady had given him was correct. Brother Glenn became the pastor of Covenant Christian Church.

I shared Brother Glenn's testimony, so you can see that God has many ways to lead, and guide us if we are willing to believe and obey. He is no respecter of persons. He has a path for each of our lives. If we will seek God, and be open to hear that still, small voice, He will speak to us. He not only speaks in that still, small voice, but He also speaks to us in many different ways.

I read once where someone had written about getting direction from God in three ways. If all three ways line up, then we can feel safe to proceed. Those ways are through His Word, His Spirit, and circumstances.

We can receive something in our heart while reading God's Word, or even by thinking on God's Word, and He will make it so real to us. Perhaps it was a call to preach after one had been reading in John 21:15-17. This is the passage where Jesus asked Peter three times if he loved Him. Peter replied that he did, and Jesus replied, "Feed my sheep". That's God speaking through His Word.

Perhaps it is a sermon we hear preached. Afterwards we feel God's Spirit on us, sometimes like warm honey, and we know it's Him. His Spirit directs us with His peace as well. Then, out of the blue, someone will say in a conversation, "You sure do sound like a preacher!" I have heard some ministers call those the three harbor lights, and they are a great guide for following God.

Brother Glenn Taylor became a dear friend of mine. I learned a lot from him. I learned about following God's Spirit in deeper ways from that great man of God. I spent many nights in his home. He came to Alabama and preached at the church I pastored. I will have more to say about Brother Glenn later, and how God used him in my life.

At the church Brother Glenn pastored in Douglas, I met a man who would also become a dear friend to me. His name was Kenny Wildes. Kenny was a big man with a wonderful smile and a contagious laugh! We struck up a friendship.

Kenny owned a business where he worked on cars. Before he died, he had tow trucks, and around 4000 auto salvage cars. He was a man of great worth but lived a simple life.

Kenny had been in the Coast Guard at a young age and was visiting NASA when the first man walked on the moon. Even then, he had favor with people in authority, and was at one of the many control panels in the control center as the moon walk occurred. Kenny was a very intelligent man. He was a successful businessman and enjoyed problem solving. Most importantly though, he loved God's Word and God's people. I had a lot of questions about God's Word, and Kenny had a lot of answers. He and I would set up for hours at night talking about God's Word. One of the things I wanted to know more about was God's Spirit, and the gifts of the Spirit. Kenny had answers!

# Chapter 5
## Baptism in God's Spirit

Not long before I met Kenny I had a customer, who was a preacher by the name of Brother Martin. He had a business in Forest Park, Georgia. He looked me square in the eyes and said to me, "Have you received the Holy Spirit since you believed?" Now at first, I was a little offended by his remark. Who does this guy think he is? It just hit me wrong for a moment, but then I realized he had said something right out of the Word of God. I was a bit confused, and I wanted some answers. God sent people in my path who had those answers. As I said in the previous chapter, one particularly important acquaintance was Kenny Wildes, from the Douglas, Georgia area. It seemed he had an opinion on most any Bible question I would ask. Kenny was a man's man, a guy you could get real with. Kenny would get real with you as well.

You know, it's interesting what people think about the Baptism of the Holy Spirit. They often want to talk about tongues. Many times, they have received some incorrect teachings. They have misgivings, and misconceptions about this amazing, empowering gift. I was one of those people. God's presence is much more than the gift of tongues but that is a good place to start a conversation.

Not long after we had met, Kenny and I were talking, and the subject of speaking in tongues in the Bible came up. Kenny asked me which of the three kinds of tongues was I interested in discussing. I did not know what he was talking about, so he explained them to me. He said that the first tongues were the ones in which the miracle was in the hearing. The Bible says, in Acts 2, that when the Day of Pentecost had fully come, then suddenly there came a sound from heaven, as a rushing mighty wind.

This was God's Holy Spirit, filling them with His presence! They began to speak with other tongues, as the Spirit gave them utterance. In verse 6, it says everyone heard them speak in their own language. It goes on to say, in verses 8 through 11, some 17 different groups of people heard the message in their own language. Yes, indeed the miracle was in the hearing.

The next type of tongues are the ones spoken of in I Corinthians 10, where a person speaks by the Spirit of God in an unknown tongue, and then what they say is interpreted. This is a sign to unbelievers, according to I Corinthians 14:22, ***"Therefore tongues are for a sign, not to those who believe but to unbelievers..."***

The spoken interpretation of a tongue should not be compared to someone speaking a phrase in another language and it in turn being translated. Translation is a word for word account of what was said. An interpretation is conveying the thought, or meaning, of what the Spirit of God is showing the one who interprets. A message given in an unknown tongue may be short, followed by an interpretation that is longer. It also may be a longer message followed by a short interpretation. It occurs that way, because the interpreter is giving the interpretation, and not a word for word translation. You see, the interpreter hears in their language, in his spirit, by the Holy Spirit, what was just spoken in an unknown language.

The third type of tongues is addressed in 1 Corinthians 14 and is concerning a believer's prayer language. This tongue is the one in which an individual prays to God and does not know what they are praying about, unless God supernaturally shows them. Their spirit prays, but their understanding is unfruitful. I believe that when an urge to pray comes on a person, sometimes life and death are hanging in the balance. We should pray in the Spirit until we get a release. Many times, our prayers will become a song when we get that release, and we will sing in the Spirit like Paul writes in 1 Corinthians 14:15, *"...I will pray with the Spirit, and I will also pray with understanding. I will sing with the Spirit, and I will also sing with understanding."*

Tongues are a way of edifying or building oneself up, almost like someone who is charging a battery. This edification is spoken of in 1 Corinthians 14:4, where the Bible says, *"He who speaks in a tongue edifies himself, but he who prophesies edifies the church."* The conjunction used in this verse is "but." It is translated many times in scripture as "and."

I believe the Spirit of God is saying through Paul that it is important for believers to pray in the Spirit and prophesy. He is not against tongues. In fact, in the very next verse Paul said, *"I wish you all spoke with tongues."* He goes on to say in verse 18, *"I thank my God I speak with tongues more than you all."* I believe Paul knew that he needed to be charged up more than anyone else. He believed in praying in the Spirit. When we are feeling low and need to be charged up, pray in the Spirit!

Paul also said in 1 Corinthians 14:5, that the interpretation of tongues is as great as prophesying.

Kenny went on to tell me that God's Spirit is a gentleman. He will not invade where He is not welcome. If we want more of God's Spirit, we must seek and ask.

Paul was in Ephesus when he asked some disciples, in Acts 19:2, *"Did you receive the Holy Spirit when you believed?"  So, they said to him, "We have not so much as heard whether there is a Holy Spirit."* In verse 5, we are told they are baptized in the name of the Lord Jesus. Notice what happened to them in verse 6, *"And when Paul laid hands on them, the Holy Spirit came upon them, and they spoke with tongues and prophesied."*

Notice, they were saved, baptized in water, and then filled with the Holy Spirit.

I think a very interesting passage of scripture is 1 Corinthians 14:39, *"Therefore, brethren, desire earnestly to prophesy, and do not forbid to speak with tongues."*

Not long before I had met Kenny, I had been wondering, praying, and seeking information and guidance about the baptism in the Spirit. It seems I do some of my most fervent praying on my feet walking. I was at home and decided to make this a matter of fervent prayer. I said to the Lord, "Father, I know you can hear me, and I know You only want what's best for me in this situation. Is the baptism in the Spirit a real occurrence? I want all I can get, so if it's real, let me know so I can receive." I heard the still, small voice of God say to me, "Go to the mailbox son."  I thought to myself, how strange that was. I was even thinking, "Did I hear that correctly?" However, I knew because I knew that I had indeed heard that, so I went to the mailbox. I reached in and pulled out an envelope. The envelope was from the 700 Club. Just in case you don't know, that's the ministry of Pat Robertson. On the front of the envelope it said, "How to receive the Baptism of The Holy Spirit!" Isn't it amazing how God answers prayers sometimes? I opened the letter and read it. You know, it's just a matter of trusting God at His Word.

Listen to what God's Word says about receiving the Holy Spirit. Luke 11:9-13 says, ***"So I say to you, ask, and it will be given unto you; seek, and you will find; knock, and it will be opened to you. For everyone who asks receives, and he who seeks finds, and to him who knocks it will be opened. If a son asks for bread from any father among you, will he give him a stone? Or if he asks for a fish, will he give him a serpent instead of a fish? Or if he asks for an egg, will he offer him a scorpion? If you, then being evil, know how to give good gifts to your children, how much more will your heavenly Father give the Holy Spirit to those who ask?"***

Perhaps you have been taught that speaking in tongues, or the gift of tongues, was a gift that lasted only for a short period of time. That it was only for when the original disciples or the apostles of Jesus were alive. However, I would like you to look at one scripture with me. 1 Corinthians 1:4-7 says, ***"I thank my God always on your behalf, for the grace of God which is given you by Jesus Christ; that in everything, you are enriched by Him, in all Utterance, in all*** *knowledge; Even as the testimony of Christ was confirmed in you: So that you come behind in no gift; waiting for the coming of our Lord Jesus Christ."* Wouldn't you say that the gift of speaking in tongues could be classified as an utterance? Let's come behind in no gift, including the gift of speaking in tongues, while we are waiting for Jesus to return.

Some people are afraid to ask for more of God's Spirit, for fear of receiving something demonic. How can we classify God's gifts to us as being evil? In the passage I quoted earlier, Jesus told us that our Heavenly father only gives good gifts. Just as we only want to bless our natural children with good things, we wouldn't give our children a serpent or a scorpion. In Luke, Jesus had sent the disciples out, and they reported back saying that the demons were subject unto them in His name. Jesus replied, in Luke 10:19, *"Behold, I give you the authority to trample on serpents and scorpions, and over all the power of the enemy, and nothing shall by any means hurt you."* From this verse, we know that Jesus was referring to demons in Luke 11:11-12. Types and symbols are common in the scripture. Jesus does not give a believer demonic spirits when one is asking for more of God's Spirit.

In James 1:17 the Bible says, "*Every good gift and every perfect gift is from above, and cometh down from the Father of Lights, with whom there is no variableness, neither shadow of turning.*"

We need to ask to be baptized into God's Spirit. I like to drink a glass of water, but one glass does not mean I am full of water. We as believers need to ask Jesus to fill us with His Holy Spirit. How can we tell if we are full of His Spirit? We will begin to speak in our heavenly language. Let's all become baptized into God's Spirit!

I have been in several Praise and Worship services where I felt like I could just lift off and go right on up to heaven. In some services, it seemed as if heaven had come down among us! The Kingdom of heaven is within us! Praise God! He is wonderful!

I wanted all of God's Spirit that I could get, so I asked Him for more, and He filled me with His presence! God is great!

Is being filled with God's Spirit a badge of arrival, or does it give us the right to brag, or make us feel that we are better than others? The answer is NO!! Receiving the baptism of the Holy Spirit is being filled with His love, which results in us as believers having a greater love for others.

I find being filled with His Spirit is a doorway that opens us up to flow in the gifts of the Spirit. It does not mean we know all things in our natural mind or have all wisdom in our natural mind, but that God's Spirit within us will lead us and direct us. Just like joining the military, this does not mean one is assigned the rank of General on the first day. Being filled with God's Spirit is a great opportunity to learn of the things of God. Why would anyone not want more of God? After all, the Spirit of God is the possessor of all the gifts. When He is present within us, as we yield to Him, all the gifts of the Spirit are there to operate as the Holy Spirit wills. The gifts manifest through us as Spirit filled believers. God's Spirit within us also possesses all wisdom and power! Invite Him in and let Him lead!

After I was baptized into God's Spirit, words that made no sense to me would come into my spirit. After a while, I would speak them aloud. It felt right, and it felt so wonderful. I would be at home or in my vehicle going down the road, and I would just feel the need to pray in the Spirit. Sometimes after praying a while, my prayers would turn into a song. I would sing in the Spirit, and joy would be in my heart. A prayer had been answered, and I did not even know what I had prayed! God's Word addresses this situation in Romans 8:26, *"Likewise the Spirit also helps in our weaknesses. For we do not know what we should pray for as we ought, but the Spirit Himself makes intercession for us with groanings which cannot be uttered."*

My friend Kenny told me that he could pray in the Spirit and balance his checkbook! Now I was not expecting to hear that! He explained to me that praying in the Spirit can become like breathing. We can do it so much that it's just that natural!

I remember once when Amber, my brother's daughter, fell off the back of a 4-wheeler. I received a phone call and was told that Amber had been taken to the hospital. Her brain was swelling. Not only was she my niece, but I was also her pastor. Amber was about 10 years old at the time. I thought I needed to go to the hospital and be with her, but the Spirit of God led me to go outside and pray. I went into the yard, and what came out of my mouth was not English. I was fervently praying in the Spirit. I knew some mighty prayer warriors, but I could not stop praying to call them. My burden was to pray in the Spirit, and I knew I was praying for Amber. Exactly what I said in that prayer, I do not know. I was being obedient to the prayer need. I wanted to go be with her, but I was very heavily impressed to pray in the Spirit.

After a while, I felt a release in my spirit. I headed to the hospital. I learned that she had died in the hospital at Haleyville, Alabama and was brought back to life. She was then flown to Children's Hospital, in Birmingham, Alabama. Now I'm sure others were praying for her as well. God heard all the prayers! However, I do wonder what I was praying in that heavenly language! Was I dispatching angels to do precisely what needed to be done? Was I binding the death angel, because God was not finished with Amber? I do not know the answer to these questions, but I do know the burden was there to pray and pray in the Spirit, and that is just what I did!

Amber arrived at Children's Hospital and walked out three days later healed! Praise God! He is so awesome!

According to the Word of God, there are three baptisms referenced in scripture. The thief on the cross was baptized. He was baptized by the Holy Spirit, into the body of Christ. This baptism is the first one and occurs at salvation. We find a reference to this in 1 Corinthians 12:13, *"For by one Spirit we were all baptized into one body..."* That body is the body of Christ.

The second baptism is the baptism in water. It is symbolic of our being buried with Christ and raised to walk a new life in Him. Matthew 2:19 says, *"Go therefore and make disciples of all nations, baptizing them in the name of the Father and of the Son and of the Holy Spirit."*

The third baptism is the baptism in the Holy Spirit.

This baptism gives us the power to walk in this new life in Christ. Jesus is the baptizer. This baptism is referred to in all four gospels. Let's look at what John the Baptist said in Matthew 3:11, *"I indeed baptize you with water unto repentance, but He who is coming after me is mightier than I, whose sandals I am not worthy to carry. He will baptize you with the Holy Spirit and with fire."* The fire referred to what happened in Acts 2:3, *"Then there appeared to them divided tongues, as of fire, and one sat upon each of them."*

In John 1:33, John the Baptist said, referring to Jesus, *"Upon whom you see the Spirit descending, and remaining on Him, this is He who baptizes with the Holy Ghost."*

Indeed, Jesus is the one who baptizes believers who ask Him in the Holy Spirit!

In the book of John, Jesus was baptized in the Holy Spirit. He came here to this earth as a man. He needed God's Spirit. After Jesus had been baptized in water, the Holy Spirit descended upon Him like a dove. God spoke out of heaven and said, *"This is my beloved Son in whom I am well pleased."* In Chapter 1, God's Miracle for Margaret, I previously talked about this verse. However, let me ask you this question. Since Jesus needed the baptism in the Holy Spirit, do you think we need the baptism in the Holy Spirit as well? My answer to that is a resounding yes!

If you remember, right after He was risen from the dead, He told his disciples that they were to go into the world and preach the gospel. However, some of the last words that were spoken by Jesus are in Luke 24:49, *"Behold, I send the promise of my*

*Father upon you; but tarry in the city of Jerusalem until you are endued with power from on high."*

Luke repeated Jesus' final words before He ascended into Heaven in Acts 1:8-9, *"But you shall receive power when the Holy Spirit has come upon you; and you shall be witnesses to Me in Jerusalem, and in all Judea and Samaria, and to the end of the earth. Now when He had spoken these things, while they watched, He was taken up, and a cloud received Him out of their sight."* He knew believers needed the power of the Holy Spirit to do the great commission, which is to carry the gospel to the world.

Some might wonder about the passage in Ephesians 4:5 that says there is one baptism. If you will notice in that same verse, it says there is one Lord. The one Lord is God the Father, God the Son, and God the Holy Spirit. This is the Holy Trinity.

Likewise, the one baptism is in three parts. Look at 1 John 5:7-8, *"For there are three that bear witness in heaven: The Father, the Word, and the Holy Spirit; and these three are one. And there are three that bear witness on earth: The Spirit, the water, and the blood; and these three agree as one."*

I believe one of the things this passage refers to is the three baptisms. The blood refers to salvation where the Holy Spirit baptizes us into Jesus. The water refers to water baptism. The Spirit refers to Jesus baptizing us into God's Spirit. What do these three baptisms bear witness to? To the supernatural. There is power available to walk a supernatural life when we walk in God's Spirit!

God's Word speaks of baptisms, being plural, in English, as well as Greek. We find this in Hebrews 6:1-2, *"Therefore, leaving the discussion of the elementary principles of Christ, let us go on to perfection, not laying again the foundation of repentance from dead works and of faith toward God,  of the doctrine of baptisms, of laying on of hands, of resurrection of the dead, and of eternal judgment."*

# Chapter 6
## A Mountaintop Conversation

Some people may think it strange that the God of creation would speak to those whom He created. Some individuals will look at you very strangely if you tell them that God told you to do a certain thing or to go to a certain place. Why??? He spoke to people all throughout the Bible. In every book of the Old Testament, there are accounts of God speaking to His children and then also throughout the New Testament. In the Old Testament, it was often through the voice of the prophet. In the New Testament, it was through His Son, Jesus Christ, and then also through the disciples and believers of Jesus. The fact of the matter is, we serve a God that is no respecter of persons. God speaking to His people did not stop when Jesus ascended into heaven. A common Biblical thread is that God speaks to His people from Genesis to Revelation.

Let's look in God's Word, starting in the Old Testament book of Exodus. We find a man named Moses, whom God was going to use to deliver His people from the hand of Pharaoh, a man who led the super power nation of the world at that time.

One would think that if God wanted to confront such a major power, He would move on a mighty nation full of valiant men and fast horses. Instead He chose to do it with a man named Moses and a stick! Now tell me God doesn't have a sense of humor!

Moses had decided early on to fight injustice by killing an Egyptian who was treating the Hebrew slaves badly. He got caught and had to leave the country.

Pharaoh's daughter adopted Moses when he was just a baby. She had found him at the river's bank, because Pharaoh had issued a decree for all the Hebrew baby boys that were born to be killed. Moses grew up in royalty but was a Hebrew at heart. God had arranged it where the woman who would nurse Moses was his own mother.

After Moses had left Egypt, he went to the back side of the desert. He spent 40 years in that place. During that 40 years God was preparing Moses for a great assignment. It would involve Moses being instrumental in the deliverance of the Hebrew children from the bondage of slavery under the hands of the Egyptians. One of the keys to that important task was God being able to talk to Moses daily.

At this point in his life, Moses was about 80 years old. How did God choose to speak to this eighty-year old gentleman? He did it in the form of a burning bush.

It is interesting to me, that Moses was just going about his day, tending to the sheep, when God interrupted his daily activities. God has a way of doing that for us if we are listening and paying attention. At odd times, He will speak to us. Moses could have seen that burning bush and thought it was quite odd. He then could have made an excuse about being too busy to check it out. He could have just said, "I'm an old man. I'm not climbing that mountain to see. It's just too high and hard." That was not the case with Moses.

There, on Mount Horeb, the bush burned, but the fire did not consume it. The source of this fire was the Angel of God! I believe Moses was visiting with the pre-incarnate Christ!

I like what Evangelist Reinhard Bonnke had to say about that burning bush. "God sets driftwood on fire. Dry old sticks can burn for God, just like Moses did! I don't pray let me burn out for Thee, dear Lord. I don't want to be an ash heap, like many of the Lord's servants who are burning out. The reason that happens is some other kind of fire. I say instead, Let me burn on for Thee dear Lord! The altar flame should never go out!"

The Lord said, "Moses, Moses!" and Moses said, "Here I am." Then the Lord said, "Take off your sandals, for the Place where you stand is Holy Ground."

Why did God tell Moses to do that? I like what Pastor Benny Knight said concerning this. He is the pastor at the church where I attend, Solid Rock Church, in Haleyville, Alabama. He said God revealed to him by His Spirit, that part of the reason God had asked Moses to take off his shoes was because of the ministry God was placing him in. Remember what the Bible says in Ephesians concerning the armor of God. It says in verse 16, ***"And having shod your feet with the preparation of the gospel of peace."***

Moses took off his shoes, and God shod him with the truth that comes only from Him. He is the one who can never lie. Whatever He speaks, happens. If He were to say all clouds are purple, then that's what they would become. His Word is perfect.

We know for sure that God was about to use Moses to write His story, and His story is one that points to Jesus.

God had many things to say to Moses. He told Moses that He is the God of his father, The God of Abraham, Isaac, and Jacob. In Exodus chapter 6,

God said that He had seen the oppression of His people in Egypt. He had heard their cry, as they suffered much cruelty under their taskmasters and knew their sorrows. He explained to Moses that He had come down to deliver them out of the hand of the Egyptians, and to bring them into a good land flowing with milk and honey. Then the Lord said in Exodus 3:10, *"Come now, therefore and I will send you to Pharaoh that you may bring My people, the children of Israel, out of Egypt."*

We can see that God had something to say. What God had to say was very important, for there were many lives at stake. The souls of men, and women, were dependent upon the outcome of this conversation. God had a plan for His people. The God of the universe had something to say. Someone had to listen, and that someone was Moses.

The God of the universe still has something to say today! Some might say, "He has already said what He wants to say in His Word." I praise God for His Word, but God still speaks by the Holy Spirit to our spirit in addition to the written Word. It is never in contradiction to what He says in the Bible. If someone says God spoke to them and it's something that contradicts the Bible, then they have not heard from God! There are many voices in the wind, and believers had better stop heeding any voice that does not line up with the Bible.

Let's say an important work is to be done through a minister who operates in the office of the Evangelist. On the same day, he is invited to two different parts of the world. He has a decision to make. In John 10:27 Jesus said, *"My sheep hear My voice and I know them, and they follow Me."*

Does it not stand to reason, that God wants to direct that Evangelist to go where he is most needed for Kingdom purpose? Maybe it's a mother trying to decide which school her children should attend. Does the school she sends her children to really matter? Does God really care? I believe it does matter! We should seek God about where we go to school, where we go to church, our jobs, and multitudes of other things in life. He speaks! He directs! God cares about every aspect of your life

Moses went on to tell God that he simply was not qualified to do the job. Moses was convinced he was not able to do what God had called him to do. God is not interested in our ability but in our availability! If we will do our part, as God leads and directs us, He will do His part through us! Moses asked God, ***"Who shall I tell them sent me?"*** God said, "***Tell them I AM WHO I AM."*** I equate this answer with the answer a parent might have to give to their children, when they ask them about doing something, and the parent's answer is "no". Then the children ask, "why not" and the parent's response is, "Because I said so!" That might not seem like a "real answer", but it is a real answer. Just as a parent establishes their position of authority in their children's lives, I believe God was letting His children, the children of Israel, know and understand exactly who He was. I believe that they were asking, "Who is the one that can deliver us from the Egyptians?" God's reply was, "I AM." Then they asked the question, "Who is able to defend us when we leave that nation?" God's reply to them was "I AM." Another question they had was, "Who is the one who can sustain us with food and clothes when we are on our journey?" God said, "I AM!"

He is the great "I AM" for the children of Israel and for His children today! He is our need supplier! We can trust Him! The Bible says He is the same yesterday, today, and forever.

God went on to tell Moses other things to do and to say. He had to obey God's instructions, as he talked to the Hebrews and then to the leader of the super power nation of the world!

Moses had an important mission, but so do we. Jeremiah 29:11 tells us that God has a plan for our life. We all have something that is important to do!! Following God's plan for our life requires that we all receive God's direction.

You might say, "Well, I will never lead a multitude out of a foreign country or do anything big." As a believer, God has great things inside of you that other people need. Let's examine how important seemingly unimportant things can be. Where would the world be if two great men of God, Dr. Billy Graham or perhaps Dwight L. Moody, had not had amazing, God loving, and God fearing mothers? What about the mother of Charles Spurgeon? What about the fathers of these men? Was the role of these parents important? Of course it was! There have been many great men and women of God with Godly parental influence who have done great things for the kingdom of God. We need God's divine direction in our lives!

Many times, and in many ways through the years, I have heard the still, small voice of God and felt His direction in my life. One such time was at an altar in Douglas, Georgia, where Brother Glenn Taylor was pastor at Covenant Christian Church.

At the Tuesday night prayer service, I had gone to the altar to seek God concerning whether I should accept the position of pastoring a church in Hamilton, Alabama. I had preached at that church for several of their services, and they needed a pastor. They had asked me to take the position of pastor. I desperately needed God's direction in this matter. The answer God gave me was not at all what I had expected it to be. As I was praying, I suddenly had a vision of a church that I had preached at a few times before in Phil Campbell, Alabama, named Bethel Baptist. I did not go to the altar with that church in Phil Campbell on my mind. It was, however, on the heart and mind of God. I was amazed to see that church in a vision as I was on my knees seeking God! There it was!

I got up from the altar and told Brother Glenn what the Lord had shown me. He said God had given him a word of knowledge for me. The word was, "oak". I was very interested to see where God was going with this.

When I got back to Alabama, I rode over to that church, and there were big oak trees all around the church. The benches inside of the church were made of oak. I was amazed. I, however, had no invitation to preach there.

I decided to not tell anyone about the vision and see what God would do. One week later, my phone rang, and it was a deacon from that church. He asked if I could come and preach. I told him I would on my first available Sunday. After that Sunday, they started asking me back to preach each Sunday. This went on for a few weeks, and then they asked me if I would come and pastor the church. I told them that I would pray and seek

God's direction in the matter.

Later that day, as I headed out in my truck, I was praying and seeking God's will and direction in the matter. I told the Lord that I knew He had given me the vision of the church. I said, "God, You may have already shown me your will by doing that, but I want to be sure. I know that you can let me know with certainty in the matter."

Suddenly, a word came in my spirit from God. The word was, "Turn on your radio son."

I must say I thought that a bit strange, but I had learned to hear His voice and knew it was Him speaking to me. I did as I was told. I turned on my radio, and it was tuned to a radio station WDJC, a Christian station out of Birmingham, Alabama. A voice came through the speakers, and a lady identified herself and said she was a member of Bethel Baptist Church!

God had my attention for sure! This was only one of several ways that God showed me to pastor that church. With God's direction and leadership, I did for 5 years.

Recently a young man in his twenties came up to me while I was attending a service at Solid Rock Church in Haleyville, Alabama. The young man's name is Josh, and he is 6 feet 3 inches tall. He is a big guy with a gentle spirit and a kind heart. He was just a child when I was pastoring Bethel, and he attended there. Josh said he was glad God sent me to that church. He believed it was for his sake. He told me he had learned the deeper things of the Spirit of God. Josh is now a mighty man of God and in the ministry! Praise the Lord!

Some people go through life and never really experience God in the way He wants us to experience Him.  God cannot be understood until He is encountered.   We need to study our Bible. The Bible is a living, breathing Word, and we need it desperately.  Prayer is an important part of our Christian walk, and I'm all for it.  However, there is something about getting rid of all the distractions, finding a quiet place, and just waiting before God. We need to listen for His voice to speak into our spirit.  Sometimes, we forget that prayer is not just about us talking to God about the situations we are dealing with.  It requires us listening for His voice and hearing that still, small voice speaking to us. As we get alone before Him, we may not experience life changing words as often as we want.  However, when God does speak or put a vision in our spirit, it can be forever life changing!

When we encounter God, we will find Him to not be a rule giver, or a God who is far away, untouchable, or stiff and uncaring.  As we come to know Him as the exciting maker of the universe who loves us, and wants to fellowship with us, then we are forever changed.  To be changed in that way, we must be willing to invite God into our world.  We must climb the mountain, so to speak, like Moses did.  He could have turned around and went home instead of climbing, and God would have used someone else.  If Moses had done that, just look what he would have missed.  He saw God's hand move in a way that no man of his generation had ever seen.

Scripture can enlighten you.  God's Spirit can draw you.  Worship can move you and make you feel good.  However, when you let Him come into your world by simply talking to Him as a friend and not in the King James English, or some preset list of words and phrases, but talking to Him from your heart, then He will change your life.   I'm talking about not only talking to Him but listening to Him and stepping out in faith on what He says to us. We learn His voice by talking to Him often.  We should enjoy being in His presence because He is with us always.  We can enjoy Him every moment. When we experience this closeness with God, we can share this with others, and then their lives can be changed as well.  You see, it's in those intimate times with God that He will lead us in what is His will for our life.  God does not want us to live here on this earth just to survive.  That is not experiencing what God has for us.  We don't need to live in survival mode but in significance mode. When we do something significant for God's Kingdom, then we can live a fulfilled life.  There are rewards in heaven for what we have done on earth.  There are crowns to be won that we can cast at the precious feet of our Lord and Savior, Jesus Christ!

  As I am writing this, I will tell about an experience I had recently.  I was in a shop, and a lady had a book on display of cards with names.  On each card, were the meanings of the names and a scripture to go along with each particular name.

  The book was open to a card that said Timmy. That is the name of a very close friend of mine. The card said, "Honoring God."  The scripture beside it was Jeremiah 29:11. It says, *"For I know what I have planned for you, says the Lord.  I have plans to prosper you, not to harm you.   I have plans to give you a future filled with hope."* (New English Translation).   After I read that, I wrote it down to tell Timmy about it.  Five minutes later, I was in another shop where a lady was telling me her daughter had moved away. She and her daughter had been running their business together. The lady, whose name is Vickie, was seeking God as to what to do next. I told her about the three harbor lights. I told her to seek God's Word in the matter for a rhema Word. She was to be led of God's Spirit, and it would be accompanied by His peace. Then she would need to pay attention to recognize circumstances wherein she should move, as God lined things up. I felt the Spirit of God come on me strong as I made the next statement.

I told her, "If you were thinking about selling the business and had a scripture as well as direction by God's Spirit, and someone walked through your door wanting to buy your shop, then you have the three harbor lights." Vickie suddenly replied that someone had done that very thing the week before. Then she said, "I know God will take care of us because He says that in Jeremiah 29:11." Suddenly, I interrupted her as she was quoting that verse, and I showed her what I had just written down with that scripture on it. She had further confirmation! You see, God does have a purpose for her life and for the people who are wanting to buy the shop as well. He knows what is best for all concerned, so we need to know what He knows in the matter! We need His direction! We need His presence! You see, her shop was not up for sale, but she was willing to listen and do God's will in the matter.

# Chapter 7
## Dreamers

When I was a boy, at approximately 12 years of age I had a dream. In this dream I had an escort. I believe this escort was an angel. It was a flying dream. I have had flying dreams from time to time, as far back as I can remember. This dream was very special. I flew over my home and around the general area. There was property across from my parent's house that stood out to me in the dream. It was one of those powerful dreams that you never forget.

Many years later, that property that stood out so strong to me in that dream was about to become available for purchase. A very sweet lady had lived there for many years. She had passed away. Her son called me and inquired if I would be interested in buying some of the property. I asked him what the price would be including the house and 5 acres of land. He said he would have to get back with me on it.

Several days later, he called me with a price. The price he quoted me was about what I thought I would pay if I were going to buy it. I asked him to give me just a few days to reply with my answer. He said he would.

I prayed about it, and I suddenly remembered the dream from my childhood. It is amazing how God weaves our lives from beginning to end if we will listen to Him and follow His leading.

I went ahead and purchased the house. It needed much repair. My father is great at remodeling and carpentry. He was the mastermind behind the project. He did most of the work on the house, working on it while I was out of town for my business.  When I would come home, I would be working alongside him as time would allow.  With help from other family members as well we got the inside finished and were able to move in!

You know, the Bible tells us about a dreamer in the scriptures named Joseph.  We find him in Genesis Chapter 37.  He was one of twelve brothers, and his father was Jacob.  Later in Jacob's life his name was changed by God to Israel.  Jacob loved Joseph more than all the other children, except for the youngest brother, Benjamin.  That made his brothers dislike Joseph greatly.  Joseph had a dream.  He told his dream to his family. His brothers hated him even more after the dream.  They already hated him, but this dream gave them ample reason to hate him more!

Joseph told them in his dream they were binding sheaves of grain out in the field when suddenly his sheaf rose and stood upright.  Their sheaves then gathered around his and bowed down to it.

Now his brothers did not say, "Bless your heart, what a lovely dream."   No, now they hated him so much that they decided to kill him.  Joseph was their father's favorite and they knew it.  Jealousy was reigning in their hearts.  Sometimes you need to use wisdom with whom you share the things that God has shown you.

God had been speaking to Joseph at a young age through dreams.  God has a way of doing this. I knew when I was a boy, even at 5 years old, that one day I would be a preacher.  God places desires in our hearts, even when we are young. God given desires and dreams can happen in your life.  However, they may take time to come to fruition as God works out the many details. Additionally, it is important that you continually seek God for His direction.  In my own life I began preaching when I was in my early thirties.

Then Joseph had another dream, where the moon and the eleven stars bowed down to him. His father, Jacob, said in Genesis 37:10, *"...What is this dream that you have dreamed? Shall your mother and I and your brothers indeed come to bow down to the earth before you?"* Then in verse 11, *"And his brothers envied him, but his father kept the matter in mind."*

Not long after he had that dream, Joseph's brothers were feeding their father's flocks in Shechem, and Jacob sent Joseph to check on his brothers.

When the brothers saw him coming, they conspired against him to kill him. They planned afterward to throw him in a pit and say to their father, "Some wild beast has devoured him."  They said among themselves, "We will see what becomes of his dreams."

One of his brothers named Reuben spoke up and said, "Let's not kill him.  Let's cast him into this pit." They stripped him of his coat of many colors, that was given to him by their father and threw Joseph into the pit.

Some Ishmaelites came by, and the brothers sold Joseph to them for 20 shekels of silver.  His own brothers sold him into slavery.  How terrible!!!

Joseph showed Godly character throughout his life.  I believe he was a man who spent a great deal of time in prayer.  Don't you know that in this situation he must have wondered in his heart where God was?  I am sure he asked God directly.

His life at that point did not make much sense, but he hung onto his faith in God.

It seemed that this was not such a good beginning for Joseph. How could it be possible that anything good could come from this? I believe Joseph just kept praying.

How many people are plagued not by their potential but by their past? How many can't go forward because of looking in their rearview mirror? One man whose life seemingly had a bad start, who was responsible for the murder of many Christians, was Paul. Today we might classify Paul as a serial killer. He could have made the excuse that God would not use him because he was guilty of murder. Not only was he guilty of murder but of the murder of Christians. However, instead of making excuses, Paul looked forward and accepted the grace of God through Jesus Christ! He wrote two thirds of the New Testament. He said in Philippians 3:13-14, *"... forgetting those things which are behind and reaching forward to those things which are ahead, I press toward the goal for the prize of the upward call of God in Christ Jesus."*

I recently read on a church sign this message, "A calm sea does not make a skilled sailor."

For many years, Joseph had a life that was full of trouble. Still, he trusted God and did not give up on his dreams.

In Egypt, Joseph was sold to Potiphar, an officer of Pharaoh and captain of the guard. God blessed Potiphar's house because of Joseph.

Potiphar's wife lied and accused Joseph of rape. He was thrown into prison. God blessed Joseph even during his time in prison. The keeper of the prison committed to Joseph the care and oversight of all the prisoners who were in the prison.

Years later, Pharaoh's butler and baker were thrown into prison as well. They both had dreams. Joseph gave each of them the interpretation of their dream. The butler was restored to his position. Joseph asked him to remember him and make mention of him to Pharaoh. Joseph interpreted the baker's dream and told him he would be executed in three days. The dream came to pass, just as Joseph had said.

One thing that was certain, was that God communicated with Joseph! Yes, God spoke to Joseph!

Two years later, the butler remembered Joseph because Pharaoh had a dream, and no one could interpret it. Joseph was summoned and went before Pharaoh. Joseph interpreted the dream. Pharaoh was so impressed that he put Joseph second in command of all Egypt. Joseph answered only to the Pharaoh himself.

Sometimes when we get a Word from God or have a dream from God, our journey does not go in a straight line. Sometimes it may seem that we are backing up, instead of going forward.

Joseph's life was full of "give up" and "go on" moments. I like this list of these types of moments given by Pastor Chris Hodges, Senior Pastor, of Church of The Highlands, in Birmingham, Alabama.    Here is a list of eleven things that happened in the life of Joseph. I would like you to examine these critical events in Joseph's life and consider how Joseph handled each situation. You can see how God brought him through these moments.

1. Misunderstood by his family................ Give up
2. Sold into slavery by his brothers......... Give up
3. Living in a strange country far from home

   Give up
4. Given favor in Potiphar's home...... Go on
5. Falsely accused by Potiphar's wife... Give up
6. Thrown into prison............................ Give up
7. Put in charge of all the prisoners......... Go on
8. Forgotten by the chief cupbearer...... Give up
9. Remained in prison two years longer  Give up
10. Interpreted Pharaoh's dream............ Go on
11. Became second in command of Egypt  Go on

What will we do in the give up moments? Did you notice there are twice as many of those give up moments, as there are go on moments? Joseph found favor in the darkest moments, because he knew his God was with him.

Sometimes we might be tempted to tell God how rough it is down here. Maybe we ask Him if He even cares. The Bible tells us that "all things work together for good, to those that love God and are called according to His purpose" (Romans 8:28). Is God the author of tragedies, accidents, or other bad things that happen to us? God forbid, NO!! However, He is more than capable of putting back together the pieces of our life upon which the devil has unleashed havoc. Often our problems are the result of us having a free will and not seeking His face before we made an important decision. Sometimes it is the things we have said and declared over our life, that don't line up with what His word has to say on the subject.

Through it all we can choose to rise above the difficulties of life and trust God to see us through. When we stand in faith believing God's word, our blessings will not be overdue a single day!

God believes in us and is hoping to see us stand on the Word and trust Him. When the devil sees that we will not be moved from believing the Word, or confessing the Word over that situation, it doesn't take him long to move on to a person who is not grounded in God's Word. We are to use our authority that Jesus gave us and rebuke the devil, in the name of Jesus, when he attacks. We are to command our ministering angels to go and bring forth what God has promised us, in Jesus' name. God will take everything the devil throws at us and make sure that we come out on top. We simply must believe His Word and trust Him!

We often pray, "God make this go away." God says, "I did not make this situation, but hold fast to my promises!" God does not use the devil to teach us. He gave us His Word and His Spirit to lead us and guide us into all truth!

God does not use sickness or disease to teach us. If He were trying to teach us something by putting sickness on us, then we would be sinning by going to the doctor to get rid of it. The Bible says He sent His Word and healed them.

James 1:2-3 says, *"Consider it pure joy, my brothers and sisters, whenever you face trials of many kinds, because you know that the testing of your faith develops perseverance."* (NIV)

Your response to offense determines your future. Joseph had the opportunity and position to take revenge on his brothers for their wickedness. The famine had brought his family back to Egypt for their very survival. As his brothers came before this great ruler, they did not know who he was. Joseph, however, knew exactly who they were. When he revealed his identity to them, they were in fear for their lives. Joseph could have had some temporary satisfaction, by inflicting great harm or death to them for what they had done to him. Instead, he recognized that God had used that horrible situation and turned it around for good.

God was able to use Joseph in a mighty way because Joseph had a relationship with Him. He showed Joseph things. When we have a relationship with our Heavenly Father, He will reveal things to us as well! Joseph had dreams.

You know, there was another Joseph that had dreams. In the book of Matthew, Chapter One, we find a man named Joseph who was engaged to Mary. Mary was not pregnant by Joseph, but the child inside of her was conceived by the Holy Spirit of God. Joseph, however, did not know this. He was ready to put her away secretly, because he did not want to make her a public example by shaming her. Isn't that a great example of the God kind of love for someone?

Look at the way God chose to speak to Joseph. Matthew 1:20 says, ***"But while he thought about these things, behold an angel of the Lord appeared to him in a dream, saying, 'Joseph, son of David, do not be afraid to take to you Mary your wife, for that which is conceived in her is of the Holy Spirit. And she will bring forth a Son, and you shall call His name Jesus, for He will save His people from their sins.'"***

I have heard some people say that you can't rely

on the information presented in your dreams. Well, God did. There are many accounts throughout the Bible, the written Word of God, where He used dreams or visions to lead His servants. He told Joseph what to do concerning Jesus in a dream! When Herod the King heard that a child was born who was called King of the Jews, he was jealous. God had already prepared Joseph by warning him in another dream. Matthew 2:13 says, *"Now when they had departed, behold an angel of the Lord appeared to Joseph in a dream, saying, 'Arise, take the young Child and His mother, flee to Egypt, and stay there until I bring you word; for Herod will seek the young Child to destroy Him.'"*

The scripture also addresses dreams in the books of Acts. The Holy Spirit had fallen on the Day of Pentecost. Believers were filled with the Spirit and began to speak with tongues, as the Spirit gave them utterance. Some thought these believers were drunk. Peter stood up and proclaimed in Acts 2:15-17, *"For these are not drunk, as you suppose, since it is only the third hour of the day. But this is what was spoken by the prophet Joel: And it shall come to pass in the last days, says God, That I will pour out My Spirit on all flesh; Your sons and your daughters shall prophesy, Your young men shall see visions, Your old men shall dream dreams."*

It is interesting that the passage speaks of dreams. God still uses dreams to speak to us. It's my opinion, that often most dreams are just dreams, but sometimes we can have a dream that's more than just a dream. Let me tell you about a dream that I had.

This dream was years ago, but it is a dream that I shall never forget. In the dream, I was in heaven. This dream was so powerful that to call it a dream seems inadequate!

In the dream I was there in heaven standing before Jesus! I was maybe 8 to 10 feet in front of Him. As I stood there, a force was flowing out of Him and into me. The force was tangible. I could not see it, but I could feel it, just like someone can feel the breeze hitting them in the face at the ocean on a windy day. It was absolutely a real force! It was amazing! I now understand more about the four living creatures in Revelation 4:8 that have six wings and are full of eyes all around and inside. They stay in the presence of God and do not rest day or night. They continually are saying, "Holy, Holy, Holy, Lord God Almighty, Who was, and is, and is to come!" These creatures are not bored! They are perfectly fulfilled being in the presence of God. There is no better place to be.

No one had to tell me what the force was that was flowing from Jesus. I knew what it was. It was 100 percent pure love! It flowed out from Him and passed through me! When I looked around heaven, there were many people there. Each one I saw, I loved with an incredible magnitude of love. It was a level of love I'd never reached on earth. It seemed, by comparison, that I had only begun to know and understand love on the earth. I could have stayed right there forever! However, after a short time, I woke up. I was forever changed, and part of me was longing for heaven. Someone else longed for heaven, many years ago.

The Apostle Paul said in 2 Corinthians 12:2, *"I*

*know a man in Christ who fourteen years ago-- whether in the body I do not know, or whether out of the body I do not know, God knows-- such a one was caught up into the third heaven."* I believe that Paul was referring to himself. In an earlier passage, Paul had been stoned. I wonder if at that time he went to heaven, but honestly, we really don't know. We do know that Paul said in Philippians 1:21-22, *"For to me, to live is Christ, and to die is gain. But if I live on in the flesh, this will mean fruit from my labor; yet what I choose I cannot tell. For I am hard-pressed between the two, having a desire to depart and be with Christ, which is far better. Nevertheless to remain in the flesh is more needful for you."*

I believe there is a longing in the hearts of God's children to be with Him in heaven. There is a crown of righteousness for all who love the appearing of Jesus. We learn this in 2 Timothy 4:8, *"Finally, there is laid up for me the crown of righteousness, which the Lord, the righteous Judge, will give to me on that Day, and not to me only but to all who have loved His appearing."* We are spiritual beings, having a human experience. We are pilgrims in a strange land, but praise be to God, one day we will be home!

I had another dream and when I woke up I knew immediately what it meant. In the dream, I was in a football game. I was playing the position of quarterback on some of the plays. I was at the receiver position on other plays. The coach in the dream told me I had to learn to play both positions well.

I never played football in High School, so this was an odd dream, but I knew what it meant. I will explain by telling a little history of my life.

After I got my heart right with God, as an adult I had a hunger for His Word. I taught Sunday School, which required me to study. I listened to Bible reading, as well as sermons, while I traveled.

You see, God had called me into the ministry. I preached at various churches. A few churches had asked me to come and take the position of their pastor, but I had no leading from the Spirit of God to do so. Something was different about the third church that asked. The Lord showed me to take the church. I was there for 5 years, as previously stated.

I had studied the Bible but had no formal training such as Bible college, or seminary. The Lord guided me, and with His help I pastored the church. Praise God, we saw people born again and rededicate their lives to the Lord Jesus. However, I still had a desire for some type of formal Biblical education.

After I was no longer pastoring Bethel Baptist Church, I received a letter in the mail. It was not addressed to me. In fact, it was supposed to go to South America. It was sent from the House of Refuge Church, being pastored by Brother Ricky White, in Haleyville, Alabama. Haleyville is my home town, as well as Brother Ricky's. It had not made it to its intended destination or had it? I believe God had it make a temporary stop at my mailbox. He had to steer it in the right direction.

I called Brother Ricky and told him that the post office had delivered this letter to me accidentally. He informed me that the envelope had a check in it and was going to South America for the work of the Lord. He asked if he could come to my place and pick up the check. I said that was fine.

The church Brother Ricky was pastoring was a Pentecostal church that believes in the full gospel message. Brother Ricky, however, did not know my opinion on being filled with the Spirit. He did not know how I believed regarding the deeper areas of God such as healing and the other gifts of the Spirit. Upon arriving at my residence, he was quite surprised when he looked at some of the books on the shelf. He said, "Brother, you have some heavy-duty books on your shelf!" I told him that I had been baptized in the Holy Ghost!

He said he was involved with a Bible College called Destiny School of Ministry. He told me they offered all levels of degrees in Biblical education.

He told me that I needed to get involved in the college. It was like something inside of me jumped when he said that. I told him I would pray about the matter, but I believe I had my answer right away.

After prayer and with the leading of God, I enrolled in the Bible College. I was out of town a lot and was able to do my courses through correspondence study as well as online.

It was not long after starting into college, while I was out on the road for my business, that the Lord gave me the football dream I told you about earlier. The Lord revealed to me the meaning of this dream the moment I awoke. When I played in the quarterback position, it was a symbol of when I had been a pastor for five years. When I played as a receiver, the Lord showed me it was my time to be taught the Word of God. God was letting me know that I was on track.

God was not yet finished speaking to me on this matter! I told no one about the dream. It was something between me and God as far as I was concerned. That would change.

I had recently started attending Solid Rock Church, in Haleyville, Alabama. It was pastored at that time by Pastor David Duncan, who had founded Solid Rock. Brother David moved mightily in the gifts of the Spirit. He would tell people, through God's Spirit, things that had happened to them and what God was about to do in their lives. Most importantly though, he preached Jesus and His love!

Brother David had preached a revival down in Douglas, Georgia. The Spirit had moved in a great way. Prophecies had come to pass from words given by Brother David, as the Spirit of God led him. The church there had invited him back for another revival.

I was attending this revival when Brother David said he had a word from God for whoever would come forward. Believe me, many did. I was just standing near the front praying, minding my own business, when Brother Glenn Taylor, who I talked about earlier in this book, came up to me and asked, "Can I pray for you?" I said, "Absolutely!" He started praying in the Holy Spirit. Suddenly he stopped and told me, "I see you in a football game." I got so excited that I immediately told him about the dream that God had given me of a football game. He told me that it was not a ball I was carrying but the Word of God!

God was giving me signs along the way that I was in His will concerning the Bible College.

Praise God for His guidance and direction!

I went on to finish 4 years of study through Bible College and received a Bachelor of Theology. To God be the Glory!

I have given the following advice to people thinking of attending college, or technical college. In our country, we elect a president every four years. It seems like those four years go by very fast. A person is one presidential term away from their life being changed by getting an education.

A few years ago, I ran into an old friend. He was in his late forties and in college, because he was studying to be a school teacher. He said, "Well I might be fifty when I graduate, but I figured I'd be fifty anyway so why not be fifty with an education!" I like that!!

I do not regret the time that I've spent learning about God and His Word.

He has enriched my life in so many ways. People have questions, and if we are familiar with the Word we can give them answers. It's great when people ask us, as believers, a question about life, or about life after death, and we can give them an answer. It's great when that answer is, "My opinion does not really matter because I can give you the answer right out of the Word of God."

There have been many times when I have been asked, "What happens when a person who is saved dies? Do they lie in the ground until the Lord's return, or do they go to heaven?" The answer to this is found in the Word. Jesus was hung on the cross between two criminals. One of them cried out to Jesus and said to Him in Luke 23:42, *"...**Lord, remember me when You come into Your kingdom.**"* Notice the response of

Jesus in verse 43, *"And Jesus said to him, 'Assuredly, I say to you, today you will be with me in Paradise.'"* We also see Paul's answer to this question. In I Thessalonians 4:13-17, *"And now, dear brothers and sisters, we want you to know what will happen to the believers who have died so you will not grieve like people who have no hope. For since we believe that Jesus died and was raised to life again, we also believe that when Jesus returns, God will bring back with him the believers who have died. We tell you this directly from the Lord: We who are still living when the Lord returns will not meet him ahead of those who have died. For the Lord Himself will come down from heaven with a commanding shout, with the voice of the archangel, and with the trumpet call of God. First, the believers who have died will rise from their graves. Then, together with them, we who are still alive and remain on the earth will be caught up in the clouds to meet the Lord in the air. Then we will be with the Lord forever."*

It is my opinion that this passage in 1 Thessalonians 4:13-17 means that a believer's body which was put in the grave at their physical death will be raised to life, but their spirits are already immortal in heaven with God and will return with Jesus to be reunited with their physical bodies, which will put on immortality when they are raised from the grave. Some people believe in "soul sleep", which means their soul sleeps in their grave with their physical body until they are raised from the grave. I do not believe that the Bible teaches soul sleep.

Another reference spoken by Paul concerning

death, is found in in 2 Corinthians 5:8, *"Yes, we are fully confident, and we would rather be away from these earthly bodies, for then we will be at home with the Lord"* (New Living Translation)

We can offer people hope in times of distress. Maybe a loved one has died, and they want to know where that person is at that very moment. It is a comfort to be able to tell them directly from God's Word.

There are many religions with many books. There are many cults. Many people claim to possess the truth of life, but Jesus is the only begotten Son of God who was crucified on a cross for the sins of the world. He rose from the dead on the third day. He is the only way to heaven. His Word is our road map for life. We will find comfort, peace, and direction in His Word when we read it and apply it daily. It's difficult to apply if we don't know it.

Sometimes, the Lord talks to us or shows us things in a dream because we are not hearing His voice gently trying to lead us or direct us. When we are asleep, God has an avenue to reveal to us something we need to know or have questions about. We have seen in His Word that dreams are important to God. The Bible says in Acts 2: 17-18, *"And it shall come to pass in the last days, says God, that I will pour out of my Spirit on all flesh; your sons and your daughters shall prophesy, your young men shall see visions, your old men shall dream dreams."* You see, God always wants to talk to us. He always has something to say. Are you listening?

# Chapter 8
## My Sheep Hear My Voice

Jesus said in John 10:27, *"My sheep hear My voice, and I know them, and they follow Me. And I give them eternal life, and they shall never perish; neither shall anyone snatch them out of My hand."* As Christians, we need to ask ourselves this question, "Do we really believe what Jesus said?" If we believe it, then we need to expect that He will do just what He said, and that He will direct us. He speaks to us through His Holy Spirit. Most of the time, it is by His still, small voice that He leads us and guides us. Yes, He speaks through His Holy Spirit. The Holy Spirit, in turn, talks inwardly to our spirit.

There are, of course, other ways our Lord communicates to us. Sometimes He uses another Christian and has them give us a word of knowledge.

Several years ago, I had a very interesting word of knowledge given to me by Pastor Glenn Taylor.

I have a good friend named Richard. Richard and I went to school together. That was many years ago, but we have always kept in touch. We live in different towns several miles away. Despite the distance in miles Richard remains a dear friend. Richard has a brother named Johnny. Johnny is a friend of mine as well.

Johnny married a lady named Judy. I would describe Judy as kind, loving, outgoing, and a fun person to be around

I was asked to pray for Judy. She was sick with two deadly diseases. One of them is what some people refer to as the "Turn to Stone Disease." It often attacks a person's major organs and causes them to harden. It can attack the heart, kidneys, liver, etc.

I was at Covenant Christian Church, in Douglas, Georgia, on a Tuesday night. It was prayer night. I asked people who were there in the congregation to pray for Judy. After we prayed, Brother Glenn spoke up and said that God had given him a word of knowledge for her. Afterward, I knew that I had my assignment. God wanted me to deliver the word to her. However, I did not want to do it. The word from the Lord was a word of correction and instruction. I knew it would be difficult to tell Judy what the Lord had spoken to Brother Glenn.

I had put off talking to her for two or three weeks. I was headed home on a Thursday evening after working out of town for four days. I was very ready to get home and get off the road. I had a praise tape plugged into my stereo and was enjoying being in the presence of God. I had decided to stop between Birmingham and Jasper, Alabama, and see Judy at her home. I figured I would read her some scripture, have prayer with her, and deliver the word of knowledge. I stopped at a pay phone to call her. There was no answer. I called her brother-in-law, Richard, and he said she was in the hospital in Birmingham. I had already passed through Birmingham, so I got back into my truck and headed toward home. I was praising God with the stereo playing all that good praise and worship music! In the middle of this time of praise and worship, I was interrupted by the still, small, inward voice of God. This is what I heard in my spirit. "Don't put another bite of food in your mouth until you go and pray for Judy."

I decided I would just go on home and fast until I could return to Birmingham the next day. I wondered what would come up the next day that would try to hinder my returning to the city. I had a business to run, an employee that would be loading a truck the next day, and details to take care of. As the miles clicked off, I had an uneasy feeling about delaying going to see Judy. I decided to take it to the Lord. I prayed this prayer as I drove down the two-lane road at night. "Now Lord, you know the situation here regarding my praying with Judy and giving her this Word from You. God, you created those stars I am seeing in the sky. You created me. You can speak to me, and I know you want me to do what's best in this situation. Lord, if you want me to go back right now, send me a sign."

As soon as I prayed that prayer, the car in front of me, which was the only vehicle in sight, turned its blinker light on. It went maybe a mile down the road before it turned. It was time to do some more specific praying.

I prayed a second time and said, "Lord, I'm asking you for a particular sign. Send me the sign of the cross, and I will turn this truck around and go see Judy!"

The Lord spoke into my spirit, "Just speak it out loud son."

I said, "Lord, give me the second sign, the sign of the cross!" There was not a vehicle in sight, but all at once an eighteen-wheeler topped the hill in front of me. I was facing the truck which had a cross lit up on the front of it! Suddenly, I felt the Spirit of God all over me! I had goose bumps as well! I turned that truck around.  I stopped at a pay phone and called Judy.  I asked her if she was up for some late-night company.  She said, "Sure, just come on over."  I had to go back the way I had just come, which was about 50 miles or so.

I walked into the hospital room and spoke to Judy's husband, Johnny.   Then, I turned to Judy and asked how she was feeling.  We talked for a short time, and I asked her if I could read her Psalms 91.  She listened intently as I read.

Next, I asked her if she understood what a word of Knowledge was.  Her comment to me was interesting.  She said she did.  She said, "I was raised in the Church of God.  I do understand."

I told her about Brother Glenn and the word of knowledge that the Lord had given to him for her.  I told her that he had said Judy had unforgiveness in her heart. She was hanging on to it.  I explained to her that she needed to let it go.  She became very emotional, and for a few minutes she did not say anything.

Finally, she spoke to me, "When I was growing up, I sang in a Christian group, played the piano, and lived for God.  At about age 19 or 20, I got away from the Lord.  Now here I am in my forties with these two diseases.  I have wasted my life.  I did not spend it serving God.  How can I forgive myself?"  Isn't it strange that the person whom she could not forgive was her own self?

There are so many people that are at that same place in their own lives.  They are not able to go forward with God.  They are too busy looking back at their past mistakes and unable to accept God's forgiveness of their own past sins.  They are often thinking to themselves, "I am not good enough.

I've sinned too greatly. How can God love me now? How can God forgive me now?" This is exactly the place where the devil wants us to be. It keeps us from going forward with God. It hinders our witness. It takes the joy out of our salvation.

I looked at Judy and asked her this question. "Does the Bible teach us that we must forgive others that trespass against us?" She agreed that the Bible does indeed say that. I asked, "Judy, are you somebody?"

It was like a light went on inside of her head. You could almost see the glow in her eyes! She responded, "Yes, I am somebody!"

I told her that to line up with God's Word, she simply had no choice but to forgive herself.

Before I left, I had prayer with Judy and then headed home. One week later, I received a phone call from my good friend Richard, Judy's brother-in-law, informing me that Judy had passed away. It was sad news. God's best for Judy, was for her to be healed here on this earth. However, we do know that when Judy walked across from this world into the loving arms of our Savior, Jesus, she received her ultimate healing! She is with Jesus, and her suffering is over forever! God's best would have been for her to live, and not die, and declare the works of the Lord. However, I do know that there are some situations where we don't see the whole picture and that we must trust God. The most important thing to know is that our heart belongs to Jesus!

Later, after I had time to reflect on the events that had transpired, I had a revelation of how God is full of grace and mercy. Every day, I am reminded in His Word of His promises, of unending love, and faithfulness towards me. Isn't it wonderful that God intervened in this situation by speaking into my spirit, and having me go right then, and there, to deliver a special message to Judy? If He had not intervened as He did, I might have been going up to a casket with a dear friend inside and stood there with a Word of Knowledge that I could not have delivered. God is so wonderful and speaks to us in so many different ways when we are listening and trusting Him.

I also want to caution you about looking for natural signs. This is sometimes referred to as "putting out a fleece", so that God can confirm or give direction into your life. Remember, Satan is the god of this world, and he can control things in the natural realm. 2 Corinthians 4:4 says, ***"In whom the god of this world hath blinded the minds of them which believe not, lest the light of the glorious gospel of Christ, who is the image of God, should shine unto them."*** We are to be led by His Spirit and His Word foremost. Will God confirm something we have received from Him with a sign from the natural realm? Sometimes He will. Often, as baby Christians, we are still learning to discern and hear the voice of God. God, in His mercy and grace, knows we need reassurance of our next step or action. However, I have found that as we grow, and develop in our relationship with Him, that the need for us to rely on natural signs diminishes as we learn to hear His voice. You see, I heard God speak to my spirit and tell me to say it out loud, "Lord show me the sign of the cross." I like what a wonderful man of God once said, that every time he had put out a fleece he had gotten "fleeced".

I believe God speaks to all of His children because that's what Jesus said in John 10:27, as mentioned at the start of this chapter. As a born-again believer, the Holy Spirit is constantly attempting to communicate to us, but it's up to us to listen. Have you ever heard that still, small voice that prompts us or directs us to pick up the phone and call someone who is sick? Or that velvety feeling of peace, when we have decided to go there or stay here? That's the voice of His Spirit my Christian friend. He wants us to follow His voice and minister His love.

In the 4th chapter of John, God's Word tells the account of a lady who had come to Jacob's well. Jesus was sitting there. She was about to draw water when Jesus asked her for a drink. She was shocked, because He was a Jew, and the Jews were to have no dealings with Samaritans. You see, Samaritans were only part Jewish and were considered to be inferior to them.

Jesus told her in John 4:10, *"If you knew the gift of God, and who it is who says to you, 'Give me a drink,' you would have asked him, and He would have given you living water."*

The woman was confused because Jesus had nothing with which to draw water. She wanted to know where He would get that living water. Jesus told her in John 4:13-14, *"Whoever drinks of this water shall thirst again, but whoever drinks of the water that I shall give him will never thirst. But the water I shall give him will become in him a fountain of water springing up into everlasting life.*

Jesus spoke of this living water again in John 7:38, *"He who believes in Me, as the Scripture*

***has said, out of his heart will flow rivers of living water."*** The King James version translates it, "out of his belly shall flow rivers of living water."

When we are full of God's Spirit that river will flow through us to give words to people in season. We need to pay attention to what is stirring on the inside of our hearts. Just listen and obey and see what God will do.

As I am writing this, I am thinking about something that happened to me recently. I was in our local Taco Bell. A mother had a little boy with her, who appeared to be about 5 years old. She looked at me and asked if I knew if the carnival had opened yet. It was in town for a few days, and since it was already Saturday afternoon, I told her I felt sure it was already going on. Suddenly, I felt in my heart I was supposed to give that little boy five dollars to spend at the carnival. I simply reached into my pocket and handed the boy five dollars. I said, "Have some fun at the carnival." I could have left it at that but seeing that we were almost in sight of the local church I attend, I told his mother, "I go to Solid Rock Church right there next to the supermarket. We would enjoy you guys coming and being in service with us." I don't know if that mom and child came to church, but I do know I followed the leading of the Lord.

Once I was in Florence, South Carolina on a business trip. It was my monthly trip there, and I often attended a church when I was there on those Wednesday nights.

On one of those Wednesday nights, I was praying and asking God where I should go to church, and He answered with a surprising response.

Suddenly, I saw in the spirit a strip mall. In this

vision, at this strip mall, was a wall. The Lord spoke in my heart and said, "Be at that wall at 7 pm, and give the person leaning against it twenty dollars." I had been coming to Florence, South Carolina once a month for the last ten years, and I knew exactly where that strip mall was. At first, I was wondering if I was hearing from God, the devil, or if it was just me!

However, when you feel that river of living water flow through you repeatedly, you will know Him more. I did, however, check myself by asking God if this was Him, and I just knew it was.

I got into my truck and arrived at the wall about ten minutes early. There were several people leaned up against the wall. I just sat in my truck until it was almost 7 pm. Then, I got out and noticed that no one was against the wall.

I started walking down the side of the wall. I passed a teenage girl who was on the pay phone. Then, after a few steps, I looked at my watch and it was 7 pm. I asked God, "Did I miss it?" I heard that still, small voice of God say to me, "Turn around son." When I did, the young lady was off the phone and leaning against the wall. She had on a McDonald's uniform. I walked right up to her, and I told her that I knew this might seem strange but that I was a minister. I explained that God had told me to come here to this wall and that I was to give the person He showed me twenty dollars at 7 pm. I handed her the money, and she replied with tears in her eyes, "Are you sure?" I said, "Yes, I am sure."

The young lady shared with me that she was expecting someone to be there to pick her up after work and to take her home. However, nobody was there. She had no ride home. The money was enough for her to call a taxi and get a ride home.

What did not make much sense at first to me, made a lot of sense to God. It sure does make our lives rewarding when we tune in and just listen to the voice of God on a day to day basis.

Back in the early 1990's, I was watching Trinity Broadcasting Network (TBN) on television. At that time, most people watched TBN on cable or on a television that picked up their local channels using an antenna. In some areas, if available, some people had those huge satellite receivers. The mini satellite dishes were just coming onto the market.

As I was watching the network on my local cable network, I heard the still, small voice of God say to me, "I want you to send TBN a check for one thousand dollars." I did believe I had heard God's voice, but I wanted to know for sure. I left out for a four-day business trip to Georgia. I prayed and asked the Lord to confirm to me that I heard Him correctly. God spoke into my spirit that He would indeed confirm it to me, and that the conformation would happen before I left the state of Georgia.

As I rode from town to town for four days, I did a lot of thinking, wondering, and praying. I remember pulling into the parking lot of my last shop on the fourth day. I said, "Lord, I still believe I heard your voice. I'll be leaving Georgia soon. I'm depending on you."

I got out of my truck and greeted my customer, whose name was Sissi. She said she needed some items and so we went to the truck. She was pulling boxes of flowers that she wanted to purchase off the shelves of the truck. As she was pulling down a box with her back turned to me, suddenly she stopped. She looked at me and asked, "Danny, do you know about those mini-satellite dishes that are available now?" I said, "Yes, I have heard about them." Sissi said, "Let me tell you what happened to me a few nights ago." Sissi and her husband were watching TBN, and the Lord spoke into her spirit. He told her to give a certain amount of money to go toward getting mini satellite dish signals into people's homes. TBN needed money for new equipment to get this job done. She then told her husband what she heard the Lord speak to her. He told her that God had spoken a figure to him as well. They decided to write their separate figures down on pieces of paper and then to compare the notes. "Danny, when we compared our numbers they were the same!" Sissi exclaimed.

This lady had my full attention at this point! I knew that God was all over this, and I needed her to go a little further with her story. I said, "Sissi, I am going to ask you a question, and I have a reason for doing so. However, if you feel it is none of my business, I will understand, and you certainly do not have to give me the answer. My question is this. What was the figure on both of your sheets of paper?" She said, "Sure, I will tell you the figure. It was one thousand dollars!" I then told her what God had spoken to me!

Praise God! He has a way of letting us know His will if we diligently seek Him. He speaks to us, and He wants us to listen!

I am including this example of God speaking to me clearly to show you how important it is to follow His voice. This example of hearing God's voice is not about how much money the Lord asked me to give, or my ability to give it. I am trying to illustrate my willingness to be obedient to the voice of the Lord. I even prayed and asked God about it before I included it here. You see, I gave to that ministry because God told me to. He blessed me greatly because of my obedience to Him. I most likely would have given to the ministry anyway if I had not had a specific amount dropped in my spirit. Now, I look around and see so many people with tv services provided by mini dish satellite providers. I can see clearly from this side of the equation why it was so important to God for that signal to go into homes all around the world. God has used the mini satellite dishes and TBN to save many souls. Through this technology, many people have been blessed through the preaching and teaching of His Word. The availability of amazing praise and worship music has blessed many people as well!

Sometimes God can speak some strange things into our spirits. He does not always say or do things the same way. When we know it's His voice, we can move on what He tells us to do. He will never have us to violate His Word, but sometimes what He speaks can be a bit odd to us.

I remember being in a service at Solid Rock Church, and the praise and worship was very intense. The Spirit of the True and Living God was moving powerfully among us.

I heard that still, small voice of God speak to me. At the same time, I had a vision. What I saw was a screen door. It was the old type of screen door that made a screechy noise when it was opened. As I saw it in the spirit, I heard the still, small voice of God inwardly say, "Ask the congregation who

82

this bears witness with. They either have one at their house, or they have recently used this specific type of door. The one who comes forward is having thoughts of suicide.

I asked our Pastor if I could say something. He handed me the microphone. I told about the screen door as the Lord had spoken to me. I purposely did not mention anything about suicide. I then handed the microphone back to our Pastor and went over to where I was standing before.

Immediately there was a lady who came forward. She said, "I'm the lady with the screen door." I told her that the Lord had shown me that she was having thoughts of suicide. She screamed and hit the floor. I was able to counsel and pray with her. I then commanded those demons that were trying to take her life to leave her in Jesus' name!

The devil can only be in one place at a time. Some might say that the devil has been after them today. In reality, I think most of us have not actually encountered Satan. We do, however, encounter his demons. A more accurate way would be to say that, "demonic spirits have been after me today."

God wants us to put those demons in their place! We have the authority of His Word on it. At times, we hear the voice of His Spirit prompting us to use our authority in situations where demonic activities are at work. The Bible tells us in James 4:7, *"Submit yourself therefore to God. Resist the devil, and he will flee from you."*

Yes, the God of the universe speaks to His children. Many of us often want a word from God, which is very understandable, but many feel it needs to come through someone else. If you are a child of God, He will speak to you.  Let's look at what John 14:17 says.  *"The Spirit of truth, whom the world cannot receive, because it neither sees Him nor knows Him; but you know Him, for He dwells with you and will be in you."*  Remember, child of God, you Know Him!!  Just pay attention to that still, small voice.  He created you for fellowship with Him.

He desires that fellowship and unity.  Unity was before salvation, and it's a powerful thing!  God had unity with Adam and Eve in the Garden of Eden. He spoke with them.  Jesus died on a cross and rose again to restore that unity.  He restores unity through salvation.  God speaks, and He will speak to you, my dear friend.

God does, however, speak through His servants to others as well.  I can remember, on one occasion, standing in front of the altar at church.  The Spirit of God was on me.  As people walked up front to the altar God gave me a word of knowledge, or word of wisdom to give to them.  I had just given a word to a lady.  Her husband, or boyfriend, who stood behind her, was looking at me expecting me to have a word for him.  It was simply not there.  If it is not there, then you don't speak it.  I prayed for him and asked God to bless him, but that was all that I could do.  We are just a conduit of God's anointing and impartation.  If we minister what He has given us, then we have done our part.  It is amazing to me when we move on what God tells us to do, and minister a simple phrase to someone, how God's Spirit at times will begin to flow and speak through us.  We can impart a living flow of words to that person from Him.  I've seen so many of God's servants operate in this way. I went for about three years, on a regular basis, to the Winston County Jail in Double Springs, Alabama, along with Pastor Benny Knight. I remember being amazed as I watched God's Spirit flow through Pastor Benny, with great power, and words of wisdom. This occurred with the men corporately, as well as individually. As Pastor Benny spoke, you could feel the very presence of God in that place. The inmates would tell us of the atmosphere being so different the night after ministry. They were sleeping better, and a calm filled the jail there because of the presence of God's Spirit.

As of this writing, Pastor Benny is still going to that jail and being used greatly of God. Many are being saved and learning to walk in victory with Jesus!

# Chapter 9
## Blessings and Curses

Moses spoke to the children of Israel before they entered the Promised Land. By the Spirit of the Lord, He told them of their God given blessings and the curses of their enemy, the devil. God told them that these curses would come upon them should they not be obedient to God. In Deuteronomy, Chapter 28, God told them, if they diligently would obey the voice of the Lord, their God, and observe all the commands that He had given to them, they would be set high above all the nations. The Lord told them that His blessings would come upon them and overtake them if they would only obey His voice. God made them many promises for obeying His word:

- They would be blessed in the city and blessed in the country.
- Their children would be blessed.
- The produce of their ground would be blessed.
- Their cattle and flocks would increase.
- Their basket and kneading bowl would be blessed.
- They would be blessed coming in and going out.
- The Lord would cause their enemies who would rise up against them to be defeated.
- They would come at them one way and flee seven ways.
- The Lord would bless their storehouses and all to which they set their hand.

- All the people of the earth would be afraid of them because they were called by the name of the Lord.

Moses warned the children of Israel if they did not obey God they would be cursed and punished. It could even result in them being exiled from the land for a time, affecting their future generations.

God warned the children of Israel to worship no other gods. This warning is found in Deuteronomy 5:9, *"You shall not bow down to them or serve them. For I, the Lord your God, am a jealous God, visiting the iniquity of the fathers, upon the children to the third and fourth generations of those who hate me."*

In our lives, as human beings, our natural heritage is an important thing. If we grew up learning about God, we are blessed. We are more likely to serve Him because of our knowledge of Him. The jails and penitentiaries are full of those who had no father figure to teach them the ways of God. I recently heard a pastor say that he believes Satan goes after the relationship a father has with his children. By making a child's relationship dysfunctional with his earthly father he can often destroy that child's relationship with their Heavenly Father, God. Without proper guidance a child can go their own direction and, just like water, follow the path of least resistance. They fulfill their own personal desires at the expense of others, and then reap the consequences of their selfishness.

I can remember my friend, Kenny Wiles, telling me of a village in Africa where elephants were causing havoc. Some experts came in and noticed that all the male elephants were young. They added older ones and the problem was solved.  It's not so simple with people, because it's not so much about age as it is the human heart. However, the foundation of our raising can make a huge difference.

Before I go further, I do recognize that each one of us has a right to make our own decisions concerning our relationship with Jesus Christ.  God does not leave us to be cursed because of a bad upbringing or not having good parents.  The choice to follow Him is up to us individually.

The Bible says, in Galatians 3:13-14, *"Christ has redeemed us from the curse of the law, having become a curse for us (for it is written, "Cursed is everyone who hangs on a tree"), that the blessing of Abraham might come upon the Gentiles in Christ Jesus, that we might receive the promise of the Spirit through faith."*

What does a person's upbringing have to do with hearing from God?  It has everything to do with hearing from God.  When a child is raised and taught the ways of God and His written word, the Bible, a child learns to hear God speaking through His Word.  Parents need to teach their children how to be sensitive to the Holy Spirit, and to be able to hear that inward voice.  This way, they will recognize the leading of the Lord in every situation. Parents have a responsibility to speak God's truths to their children.  Be thankful if Godly parents have raised you, and you have been taught in the knowledge and fullness of God.  If that wasn't the way you were raised, just commit right where you are to pass on a Godly heritage to your family, loved ones, and friends.

I can remember having conversations about

generational curses with my friend, Kenny Wiles, who went to heaven several years ago. Kenny had an interesting thing happen in his life concerning generational curses. I think it is a great example of how curses work, and how demons try to use them to rob, steal, kill and destroy.

Kenny had a wrecker business and an auto repair service. He received a call one day to go and pick up a vehicle that had been wrecked. When he got there, the driver had been the only one in the car. Kenny got the wrecked car secured to transport it and took it back to his business. After arriving there, the young driver came into Kenny's office. Kenny said he perceived by the Spirit of God to talk to this young man. First, he told the young man about Jesus. Kenny's business was his pulpit! We need more men like Kenny in the world! He asked the young man if he would like to invite Jesus into his heart. The young man said "Yes!" Kenny then led him to the Lord. Praise God!

Kenny heard in his spirit that he needed to question the young man about generational curses. He asked if the young man knew what they were. He did not know. Kenny said, "Let's say for example, if your grandfather was an alcoholic, then chances are your father would be. Then, it could pass on down the line to you." Kenny kept going and said, "Now for another example, if your grandfather were to have been suicidal, or struggled with suicidal thoughts, then most likely your father would suffer with those same demons. You, too, would most likely battle similar issues."

After finishing his explanation, Kenny said, "I feel that we need to pray and break generational curses off your life. We want to claim your freedom in Jesus!" That's exactly what they did.

The young man's grandmother was standing outside of Kenny's office and overheard the whole conversation. After the young man walked out, she walked in. She asked Kenny if he knew their family and their situation.

Kenny told her that he did not. She said that the young man's grandfather was her husband, and that he was an alcoholic. The young man's grandmother then said that he killed himself. She then went on to say that the young man's father was her son. He was an alcoholic, and he, too, committed suicide.

That young man had been a small boy and was in the same house, when his father took his own life. He used a gun.

Grandma was rejoicing in the salvation of her grandson. They believed that the young man, who was battling demons of alcohol, was trying to end his own life in that car.

Kenny had done a lot of jail ministry. In almost every situation where he had ministered to and prayed with an inmate, he had perceived in his spirit that there was a need to break generational curses. He said it was so often that he prayed and questioned God concerning it. The Holy Spirit revealed to Kenny that individuals that struggle with life controlling issues have a great need for generational curses to be broken over their lives.

Indeed, people need to be free. I'm glad Jesus came to set the captives free! "Whom the Son sets free, is free indeed!" We need to recognize, claim, and walk in that freedom!

I'm thankful to God because I was blessed to be

raised by Christian parents.  My father is as honest a man as I know.  His word is his bond.  His map is his Bible.  Jesus is His Lord.  He is not shy about telling others right from wrong.  We need more people in this world like him, who are willing to stand for what is right based on God's Word.

I am very blessed that my dad is still living and able to do daily exercises that would challenge many people that are half his age.  He is in his early 80's as of this writing.  I have many memories of him throughout the years.  He would be in his chair with his Bible in his hands, reading and studying God's Word.  As a young man, when my father shared what he was studying, I heard God's voice through my father.

My mother is in her 70's.  She is a blessing.  She is the kindest person that I have ever known.  I'm sure I am biased about her, but others that have known her through the years say similar things about her.  She is more concerned about others than she is for herself.  She is full of the love of Jesus.  " All of her children rise up and call her blessed," because she is a Proverbs 31 virtuous lady!  I am blessed!

My mother's daddy, my granddaddy, was Velmon Shirley.  He was a coal miner.  He loved Jesus and referred to Him often as "The Good Lord!"  My granddad loved to fish.  I can remember as a boy going to the store and hearing him talk to the person behind the counter about the Good Lord!

My granddaddy never claimed to be a preacher, yet he had started a church.  He had services in his home and would get a preacher to come and speak.  Out of this, someone donated some land for a church to be built.  One day, he was at that property laying blocks, and the preacher came by. He said, "Brother Shirley, you are out here all by yourself working. This is too much. Maybe you should give up on this since you have no help." He replied, "Preacher, if one soul gets saved it will be worth it all. I believe I'll just keep on working."

That church building was completed and many, many souls have been saved there, one of which was my father. The church is now over sixty years old. The church building has had additions and improvements, of course, but those blocks he laid are still there, along with the other physical work which he did on the building. The name of the church is Unity Baptist, and it is located in Bessemer, Alabama, in the Concord community. God has blessed the church through the years.

Before my Granddad passed away, he asked me to record a message for his family and then play it for them after he died. The funeral was over, and we went back to his house. I told the family that Grandad had left them a message, and his desire was that we all listen to it together. I turned on the cassette tape player and he said, "I want all my family to love God, love one another, and get along. I want us all to be together in heaven."

What a powerful statement! That was his heart. God, family, unity, and love for others! The family does get along, and most all are in church every Sunday and love the Lord. What a heritage he and my Mamaw left behind, because of their love for Jesus, family, and others.

During their lives, my Granddad and my Mamaw sowed much love in their community. She often cooked food and carried it to those who were sick, or those who had recently had their loved ones pass away.  They were a great couple who loved God.

My Mamaw was born Rosie Gunnels.  Her father was John Gunnels.  In approximately 1917, when John Gunnels was a young father with 6 children, his wife became ill.  The doctor told them that she would die.  She told her husband that the three youngest children could not even get themselves a drink.  She said that she would carry them with her to heaven when she died.  Despite everything the doctor tried, not long after she died, the three youngest children died as well.

After these events, my great-grandpa Gunnels never married again and became a hard man. He was a farmer.  He would have the family waiting in the fields for the sun to come up in the mornings. It seemed life had dealt him a tough hand.

My mother tells the story of what happed when great-grandpa Gunnels was an old man.  His son-in-law, my granddad Shirley, invited him to go to a revival service.  He decided to go.  He was old and walked with a cane.  My mother said she will never forget when the invitation was given.  Great-grandpa took her by the hand and said, "Walk with me to the altar."  He gave his heart to Jesus!  Not long before he died, my mother said she and my Mamaw were standing outside of his bedroom door.  They could hear him singing the song, "I'll Fly Away!"  That story is really a blessing!  He died before I was born, but I will see him one day.  He gave his heart to the Lord and became a fellow believer!

Glory to God!  He is in heaven with his wife and those babies that he buried.  Praise God!  That makes me want to shout!!!  Troubles will come, but when we are in Jesus Christ, better days are coming!  Just like Paul said in 2 Corinthians 2:14, "*We always triumph in Christ Jesus!*"  That means we always win, regardless of the situation or circumstances.  Jesus gave us the victory!!!

I heard once at a church folks were getting up and each quoting their favorite Bible verse.  One old gentleman stood and said, "My favorite verse is the one that says, "And it came to pass!"  Praise God, there is something to that!  If you are in a test or fiery trial, child of God, just hold on to the promises of God because it did not come to stay!  Jesus has given us the victory!!!  *"We are more than conquerors through Him that loved us,"* according to Romans 8:37.  It would be good enough if we were just conquerors.  However, the Bible says we are more than conquerors.  Not only do we win in every situation, but it is an abundant victory.

The last grandparent of mine to pass away was my dad's mother.  Her name was Elvie Brooks.  She was a no-nonsense kind of lady who loved God and expected people to do what was right.  If you were wrong, Granny would tell you that you were wrong.  She was full of faith and love.  She was a poor sharecropper, tending cotton fields much of her life.  I heard my dad say once that he would have starved to death had it not been for his mother.  She knew how to make do and stretch what little she had when her children were growing up.

Granny brought five children into the world.  All five made the decision to follow Jesus Christ.  She instilled the most important value into them!

About two or three years before she died, the

doctors had given her up. We prayed the prayer of faith over her in the name of Jesus! The doctors had discovered she had a problem with the arteries in her heart. To the amazement of the doctors, her body produced new, extra veins! Praise God! He performed a miracle! Granny was in her eighties when she passed away. Two of her grandsons, Dr. Chris Fuller, and myself, were honored to preach at her funeral. I was blessed to be able to speak at all three of my grandparents' funerals, with divine impartation from the Holy Spirit. The only grandparent whose funeral I didn't preach was my Dad's father. He died when I was two years old. Sadly, I didn't get to know him.

I share all of this about my grandparents to say how God used each of them in my life. They spoke truth and imparted much wisdom into me. I also want to stress the importance of living for God. We should serve Him cheerfully, and with a willing heart, especially before our children. It should be every parent's desire to leave their children an inheritance. It is truly wonderful to give them the inheritance of a life of faith and trust in our Heavenly Father. Knowing Him, loving Him, and serving Him is more valuable than any material blessing we can leave our children.

# Chapter 10
## Godly Wisdom from A Friend

I have already mentioned Kenny Wildes, my friend from the Douglas, Georgia, area. I learned a lot about God and the Holy Spirit from Kenny. Kenny was all about doing what he could to put himself in a position to hear God's voice.

His close walk with God had been birthed through tests and trials. The demon spirits do not want us, as Christians, to hear the voice of God. They will try in every way they can to prevent our fellowship with God. My friend Kenny has since gone to be with the Lord. I would like to share some of his story. I share his story to show you the importance of learning who we are in Christ. We must learn to rise up and use His Word to fight the devil and demons. Let's go forth in victory in Jesus' name!

Kenny joined a church that did not teach or believe in the Baptism of the Holy Spirit. He joined the Brotherhood, drove a bus, taught Sunday school, was involved in visitation, and even joined the Gideons. His personal business was going well so he was happy with life. He said he was totally ignorant of spiritual warfare. However, he soon became educated in fighting demonic forces.

Kenny found himself with financial problems and family problems. He lost his family and buried himself in his work. God's Spirit was pulling at him, but Kenny kept slipping further away from God. God has a way of getting the attention of His children.

The Sheriff's office called Kenny, who was in a neighboring county, to tow in a large tractor/trailer rig with his big wrecker. The driver had been dead in the truck for about 4 or 5 days.  The truck was locked up, and the man had decomposed in the sleeper cab very badly.  Kenny got the job of cleaning the truck up.  It was a new truck.  He had to remove and replace all of the interior.

Kenny contacted the dead man's brother in Orlando, Florida. The brother wanted all of his belongings to be shipped to him in Orlando.

As Kenny was going through the items, he was shocked to discover that the man was a Satan worshiper.  There were all kinds of satanic materials in the truck.  He also found a letter the dead man had written to his wife, telling her that he wanted to get out of this way of life.  He did not live to finish the letter, so Kenny concluded that the demons had killed him.  Kenny informed the brother that he would not ship the satanic stuff.  The man's brother told Kenny that he would be sorry if he did not send those satanic materials to him.  Kenny decided to burn the items.

Shortly after disposing of the satanic material, Kenny had strange things start to happen in his life.  He was a big man, yet he became scared and nervous.  He felt like someone was always looking over his shoulder.  Fear turned to panic, and he got scared to even go near the truck.  He tried to wash away the feeling with much water and soap, but it would not leave.

Then the threatening voices started.  He would not even go back into his own building at night.

Kenny said he talked to three different preachers about the problem, but they were of no help to him. They just basically asked if he was okay.

At night, he would try to sleep.  He said the demons would jump out and throw daggers and knives at him.  Kenny was wide awake in his bed and ducking these attacks.  He kept every light in his house on all night long.  After one week of these strange occurrences, he said he was so crazy.  He now understood why people go into insane asylums or suffer nervous breakdowns.

Kenny told me that he got so desperate, that he mentioned what was going on to someone at work. Kenny owned an auto repair business.  It turned out that this employee knew a man named Bobby Moore.  Brother Bobby was a Pentecostal preacher, and Kenny said he was willing to talk to the man.  Kenny was not a member of the Pentecostal church, but he had to have some help! The employee arranged for Brother Moore to come to Kenny's office.

As Kenny explained to Brother Moore what was happening to him, Brother Bobby just smiled and said, "I know what is happening."  Brother Bobby then decided to wait until there were no customers in the building so that it would only be him, Kenny, and the other employees there.  Brother Bobby got out his Bible and anointing oil.  Then Brother Bobby went to the truck once driven by the deceased man, read the Scriptures concerning the believer's authority in Christ, and anointed the truck with oil.  He did the same with Kenny's building, as well as Kenny, and his employees.

Kenny said when Brother Bobby was done, it was as if someone had gone over and flipped a light switch on!  You see, Brother Bobby knew who he was in Christ!  He was exercising the authority that was given to believers by Jesus in Mark 16:15-18, *"Go into all the world and preach the gospel to every creature.  He who believes and is baptized will be saved; but he who does not believe will be condemned. And these signs will follow them that believe: In My name they will cast out demons; they will speak with new tongues; they will take up serpents; and if they drink anything deadly, it will by no means hurt them; they will lay hands on the sick and they will recover."*

Kenny had actually been suffering from demonic attacks for years, but this intense attack had lasted for a week. He had been having nightmares for years. He realized two weeks later that they were gone.

After everything that happened, Kenny decided that he would make a rededication of his life to the Lord and get back on track with Him. He said he was sitting in his easy chair, and he said to the Lord, "I'm back. Where do I start?" At that moment, he got a startling revelation from God. The voice was not audible, but it was just as if someone were speaking to him. The Lord said, "I can't use you. You don't know My Word." Kenny was shocked but knew it was true. His recent experience had taught him that.

Kenny told me that the Lord showed him that in the past he had been trying to worship Him under a spirit of religion. The Lord showed him that he was more interested in works and concerned about what men thought about his performance than what God thought.

He prayed and told the Lord that he had a hard time understanding the Word. Often, he would fall asleep trying to study even before he had finished one chapter. He asked God to give him a desire for the Word and an understanding of what he was reading. He told God that he was willing to put forth the time and effort to learn the Word of God.

Kenny told me it was like an explosion took place in his heart and mind. Suddenly, his greatest desire was to study the Bible! He studied early, late, at lunch, and on the job. It was like the Bible had changed for him. He said it was almost like someone had rewritten it overnight!

Kenny knew it was important that he get back into church, but he realized it would have to be a different church. He went past the church Brother Bobby was pastoring and the Lord said, "Go back." Kenny said there was a battle within himself about going into this church, because it was a Pentecostal church. God won, however, and Kenny started attending.

Kenny began to learn about spiritual warfare. He asked God why he was getting so much revelation on the subject. Kenny didn't see himself as a minister. He believed he had not been called to be a preacher. He heard God speak into his spirit, "Because some in the ministry won't minister the whole truth, I'm going to the lay people." At first, Kenny was angry at the Christians he knew for not teaching the whole truth. He wanted to challenge all of them to discover how necessary it was that the whole Bible be preached.

God quickly set him straight on this. He showed Kenny that most Christians were just like him. They were busy working so they could feed their families and get through life. The devil and his demons had lied to them too, and they really did not understand the authority given to them by Jesus. Kenny heard in his spirit that they were born again Christians who had not allowed their spirits to grow. Some had not fed their spirits by studying God's word. Many people had worshiped Him with their minds and had been deceived by the deaf and dumb spirits. They had not learned how to spiritually discern the Word. They did not perceive that as believers God wanted us to worship Him with our spirits, as well as our souls and bodies. Jesus said in John 4:24, ***"God is a Spirit; and they that worship Him must worship Him in Spirit and in truth."*** The Lord put it in Kenny's spirit to be patient with them.

Kenny noticed that people who were full of God's Spirit, were led by His Spirit and had a peace and assurance that other believers did not have. Just like a lot of Christians who have been raised in traditional denominational churches, Kenny was quite skeptical of Pentecostal believers. He had been taught that speaking in tongues was wrong. He had not seen that Pentecostal believers had an understanding and knowledge of the fullness of God's Holy Spirit, and His amazing gifts.

God was teaching him. Kenny learned to put on a new nature of love and compassion for others. He learned that the more we trust and obey Him, the more we take on the nature of Jesus.

Kenny wanted to learn about flowing with God's power and walking in the authority that Jesus has given the believer to overcome every demonic force. His desire was also to teach others how to walk in that level of authority. The Lord showed him that this new level would involve his being baptized in the Holy Ghost, with the evidence of speaking in tongues. Kenny had been taught all his life that he did not need this. He knew he could get to heaven without being filled with the Spirit, so why bother?  He was also worried about getting some kind of evil spirit, instead of the Holy Ghost.

Kenny heard God speak into his spirit to just trust Him and be led of His Spirit.

Immediately, the devil chimed in and said, "You can't have what these people have.  You can't be anointed or baptized with that power from the Holy Spirit."  The devil quickly began reminding Kenny of all his faults.  Remember, the Bible tells us in Revelation 12:10, that the devil is the accuser of the brethren.

He was still in the middle of a divorce, and the devil tried to tell him that he could not be blessed of God and receive His power.

You see, Satan knows that when a believer gets baptized in God's Spirit, they will rain on the devil's parade.  The demons know and tremble at the boldness that rises in a spirit filled believer! Kenny Wildes wanted that power.  He was ready to exercise his authority over the devil and walk in victory through Jesus.

As Kenny studied, he learned that he needed to totally surrender to God. He had to let go of religious teachings and be led by God's Word and His Spirit.  He had to believe what was in the Bible and quit trying to change it to suit his old beliefs.

One night, Kenny was attending a revival.  The evangelist who was ministering said, "If you are not walking in God's power, and if you want to be anointed with the gift of the Holy Spirit, the first thing you must do is to ask God in faith."  The gift of the infilling of the Holy Spirit is free, just like salvation, but it does require action on the part of the one wanting to receive. That action is to ask, believe, and receive.

Once again, the devil began telling him why he was so unworthy. He then heard a voice that was firm but full of love. It was God's Spirit saying that the gifts are for the perfecting of the saints, not for perfect saints. Kenny got into the prayer line and let them lay hands on him and pray. As they were praying, he could feel the presence of God from his head to his feet. Kenny was overcome by this beautiful feeling. It was so great that he began to stagger, like one who was drunk. Remember in Acts 2:15-18, when the Spirit of God fell on the believers some thought they were drunk on wine. In fact, they were drunk, but not on alcohol, they were full of God's love and His Spirit!

The peace and power of the Holy Spirit filled Kenny's mind and spirit. It was as if he was under a fountain of water. As they prayed, he began to have a strange but peaceful experience. His mouth began to move and speak. As he yielded and allowed it to continue a strange language began to come out. He was no longer afraid of it. He began to flow with the Holy Spirit in his spirit.

The next day, Kenny was called out on a wrecker call. Once again, evil spirits bombarded his mind. They tried to convince him that he did not receive the baptism of the Holy Spirit. They tried to tell him that he looked foolish in front of all those people. The evil spirits told Kenny that the church members were laughing at him. They whispered, "Look, you are a big man, and there you were laying on the church floor like a little wimp."

This time, as those thoughts came into his mind, a new feeling rose up inside of him. In his spirit he began to pray. He asked God if what he experienced was real, or if he had gotten caught up in the moment and just had an emotional occurrence. Suddenly, the cab of that wrecker was filled with the presence of God's Spirit! That beautiful feeling of peace came over him, and tears began to flow down his face. He could not control the tears. The joy was so great that he thought his heart was going to pound out of his chest! Kenny realized that what he had been fighting all those years was so sweet and wonderful! He had been filled to overflowing with God's Spirit and love!

The more he prayed in the Spirit the prayers just came more and more naturally.

Kenny used his testimony to win others to Christ. He shared the plan of salvation along with his powerful testimony. One day, he witnessed to someone who was an alcoholic. Later that night, he came under demonic attack. He felt like he was being smothered in his bed. He felt a choking around his neck. He tried to call for help but could not speak. He was paralyzed and could not move. Kenny felt like he was dying, and panic was about to set in. He said he could not help himself.

Then suddenly, Kenny's spirit began to pray in the Holy Spirit. The more this happened, the more the demons turned loose. He got free and ran from his house. He was really praying in tongues at this point! He bound those demons in the name of Jesus! The Lord later showed Kenny that he had failed to cover himself under the blood of Jesus, and that had allowed that man's demons to attack him.

After that, Kenny had no doubt what the Holy Spirit was trying to show him about the power of praying in the Spirit. The gifts of the Holy Spirit have a purpose. The Holy Spirit speaks to our spirit and gives us His leading to pray.  Perhaps we are praying for a friend, or family member.  We may not know for whom we are praying but that's okay.  When we feel this prayer burden in the spirit, it's time to pray!   It's very important.  Life itself may be on the line.

Kenny learned that there is power in the blood of Jesus, the name of Jesus, and praying in the Spirit! He learned that we must exercise our spiritual authority over demonic forces and evil spirits.  He also learned we need to plead the blood of Jesus over our lives, the lives of our children, and any difficult situation in which we find ourselves.

We can claim that power of the blood of Jesus over our minds, homes, churches, businesses, and so forth.  We do not have to fear the demons because the demons fear the Blood of Jesus!

I learned another lesson from Kenny, and I have applied it many times since then.  Kenny told me about one time when he was in a service. The Spirit of the Lord came upon him and told him to shout.  Kenny said he was reluctant to do so and did nothing.  The Lord impressed him further and he obeyed.  As he did, he was suddenly in the spirit realm.  He could actually hear what the lady behind him was thinking.  He said she was thinking, "I wish that fellow that's shouting would just shut up!"  At the same moment, it was like Kenny was on the balcony.  He could see himself below.  He saw himself shouting, and the blood of Jesus was coming from his mouth.  As it did, demons were being dislodged from people all over the sanctuary.

After learning this information, there have been many times in my life that I have been in a worship service and it would seem just to be a normal service. Then the Spirit of God would come upon me and tell me to shout! I can say that without exception, I've obeyed the Lord many times in this. As I have been obedient to act on what the Lord said to me in this, the service has gone to another level. I have seen people leave their seats, come forward to pray, and receive Jesus into their hearts! I believe that by my act of obedience the Spirit of God was loosed. The demons were driven back, which allowed the people the freedom to run to Jesus. My prayer is that each person who reads this will remember this truth forever!

Praising God will still and stop the enemy in its tracks. I encourage you to step out and see what happens. If you are not normally a shouter, just do it if God directs you. You will be amazed. The lives of people will be changed because of your act of obedience.

I remember once being in a meeting at a place called "The Ramp" in Hamilton, Alabama. The Ramp is a ministry that was founded by Karen Wheaton, an anointed singer and teacher. Someone behind me was being loud but they were not in the Spirit. It was beginning to bother me. After listening to this for some twenty minutes or so, I started to pray. I said, "In the name of Jesus, I loose angels in this place to shut this discord down. I bind the demons in Jesus' name and command you to stop." Now I did not do this loudly, but softly. Immediately, the chaos stopped! You see, the Spirit of God showed me that there was demonic activity trying to disturb the service. The Bible teaches us that there is power in the name of Jesus. We need to know who we are in

Christ, rise-up, and exercise our God given authority!

In the book of Acts, Paul and Silas encountered a situation where they were traveling and preaching the Gospel. A demon was harassing them. The demon was operating through a slave girl. It was a demonic spirit of divination. She brought her masters much profit by fortune telling. The girl followed Paul and cried out in Acts 16:17, *"...These men are servants of the Most High God, who proclaim to us the way of salvation."* Apparently, she was doing this in a sarcastic tone. She was not for them but against them.

Finally, Paul being led by the Spirit, took his authority in Christ, and dealt with the possessed girl. We find out what happened in Acts 16:18, *"And she did this for many days. But Paul, greatly annoyed turned and said to the spirit, 'I command you in the name of Jesus Christ to come out of her."* He came out that very hour.

That spirit was so removed from her that her masters saw that their hope of profit was gone. Afterward, they seized Paul and Silas and dragged them before the magistrates. They were beaten and thrown in jail. In jail they praised God by singing hymns to Him. God sent an earthquake and opened all the prison doors. The jailer, fearing that the prisoners had all escaped, and that he would be held accountable, decided to kill himself. However, Paul called to him and said, *"Do yourself no harm, for we are all here."* (Acts 16:28) That jailer fell down before Paul and Silas and said, *"Sirs, what must I do to be saved?"* (Acts 16:30) They said, *"Believe on the Lord Jesus Christ and you will be saved, you and your household."* That jailer got saved, brought Paul and Silas into his home, and fed them!

Paul knew the power that was in the name of Jesus over the demonic forces. We need to understand and walk in the power that we have in Jesus' name.

There are two other important spiritual truths here. This passage shows us what to do when we are in a difficult situation, or facing "a prison type experience", or at the midnight hour when all seems lost. If we will lift our voices in prayer and praise, then thank God for all that He is doing in our life, He will turn our situation around. Praising God changes things.

The other truth seen here is that often in a Christian's life when things aren't going our way, or trouble comes, we tend to think that we have missed God. The devil lies to us and tells us our troubles are the result of us not being in God's will. If Paul and Silas had been like a lot of Christians, they would have been moaning and complaining about ending up in jail after they had been doing God's work. Silas might even have thought that Paul had missed God and that's how they ended up in prison. A friend of mine once asked an instructor at Bible College if bad things are happening in your life does that mean that you are out of the will of God? The instructor laughed and said, "The devil attacks people who are actually a threat to his kingdom. You can be right in the exact place where God wants you to be, and the devil wants to stop you from reaching people."

I challenge each of you who read this to follow the leadership of the Spirit of God in church services. Do what He tells you to do and see what happens. During the preaching, and particularly during the invitation to accept Jesus, command the demonic spirits to be mute in Jesus' name. That will shut them down and free up the lost person's mind so they can make the most important decision in their life, to accept Jesus as their Lord and Savior. The decision, of course, is up to the person who is under conviction by the Holy Spirit. They can accept or reject a relationship with Jesus. It is up to us to intercede, do our part, and bind those demonic voices that are trying to influence them negatively.

# Chapter 11
## Angels Among Us

In 2 Kings, chapter 6, we find a prophet named Elisha. The king of the nation of Syria was on a manhunt for Elisha. You see, Elisha was telling the king of Israel inside information about the plans of the king of Syria. The interesting part is that this information was coming from God. Of course, God knows all things. One of the king's servants told the king in 2 Kings 6:12, *"...Elisha, the prophet who is in Israel, tells the king of Israel the words that you speak in your bedroom."*

Now, the king of Syria asked where Elisha was. He wanted his men to go and get him. The king was informed that Elisha was in Dothan. He sent horses, chariots, and a great army to Dothan. They came at night and surrounded the city.

Elisha had a servant who saw this great army early the next morning, and he was afraid. He asked Elisha, "What shall we do?" We pick up with what happened in 2 Kings Chapter 6:17-18, *"And Elisha prayed, and said, Lord, I pray thee, open his eyes, that he may see. And the Lord opened the eyes of the young man; and he saw: and, behold, the mountain was full of horses and chariots of fire round about Elisha. And when they came down to him, Elisha prayed unto the Lord, and said, Smite this people, I pray thee, with blindness. And he smote them with blindness according to the word of Elisha."*

The servant's eyes had been opened to see into the realm of the Spirit. The angels were already there but the servant could not see them until his eyes were made to see into that supernatural realm by God.

We live with a limited perspective of things in our natural environment. We look into the night sky, see the stars, and much darkness. I've often wondered what it will look like when we are passed from this life and live in the spirit realm. I believe what we see looking into outer space will be much different than the perspective we now have.

If hundreds of people would have been with Elisha, they also would not have seen what Elisha's servant saw unless God allowed it.

I had a peek into the spirit realm, and I will share that event. It's one I will never forget.

I had gone over to visit with some friends. They had been having some difficulty in their marriage. She had left him and took most of the furniture. She had not heard from him in two weeks, and that was the situation into which I had walked. He had remained at their home but believed that if she got ready to come back, she would simply just come back. He was not going to call her and ask her to come back. He had prayed and was trusting God for the outcome. I'm not saying I agree with his strategy. I am just relaying what happened. However, in this case it worked because there she was, back at home.

I talked with them both for a while and then, before leaving, I asked if we could all three pray. They agreed, we joined hands, and began to pray one by one.

As I was praying, I suddenly became aware of an angel standing by us. He was a very tall angel. He was an angel of war. He had a sword in his hand, and he was stabbing it into the floor. Now afterward, there was no damage to the floor. One might say, "Did this really happen?" Just listen to the rest of the story!

Every time the angel stabbed the floor it was very loud, and the sound reverberated around the room. Angels come for a purpose and this was no exception. Following a few stabs with the sword, the message of the angel was, "What God has joined together let no man put asunder." I was amazed and told the couple what I had witnessed. They had seen nothing.

Suddenly, the lady said she perceived in her spirit that we were to partake of the Lord's Supper. I said, "I sense in my spirit that we need to do this as well. We also should put bread and juice outside and inside the home, to redeem the land and property."

As I recall this situation, it puts me in mind of King David. He was in a fierce battle, and he made the statement, "Oh that someone would give me a drink of the water from the well of Bethlehem, which is by the gate!" Three of David's mighty men broke through the camp of the Philistines and drew water from the well. They brought it to David. David did not drink it but poured it out unto the Lord. David said in 2 Samuel 23:17, ***"Far be it from me, oh Lord, that I should do this! Is this not the blood of the men who went in jeopardy of their lives? Therefore, he would not drink it. These things were done by the three mighty men."***

At the couple's home we then took communion. First, the lady went outside, poured some juice and bread on the ground. Then, we came inside, and she put bread and juice on the floor. When many of us think about the juice in the Lord's Supper, we think of a very small cup. Her cup was not small, and she had a lot of juice in it. The floor in the house was hard, it was not carpet. She poured the juice out and it formed a sword. It was as if you were drawing a sword with juice instead of a pencil. It had a handle and a thirty-six-inch blade. I actually measured the size of the blade. The lady wiped up the juice with a towel. It was an experience that none of us would ever forget. The point was clear. God wanted this couple to stay together! They did, in fact, stay together.

Before I left this couple's home, the lady's eyes were opened, and she saw and described the same angel that I had just seen. God can get very real with us when we get real with Him. Not long after this happened, the husband died. How sad it would have been for this household to have been broken apart! Imagine the guilt and pain that wife would have felt.

Another time in my life when I experienced angelic intervention occurred when I was about 19 years old. However, I was not living for the Lord at that time. I was in a car going down the road adjusting the car's tape player. I was not paying attention to my driving as I should have been. My car ran off the road. I should have simply eased it back onto the road. It did not want to go, and so I just jerked the steering wheel and I lost control of the vehicle. The car went completely across the road, and I was headed off the highway where there was a huge drop off. There was a bridge nearby, but the car's momentum was not carrying me towards the bridge. My car was headed in a direction that would put me totally missing the bridge, going off the side of the highway, and plunging to the bottom. I was so out of control that there was nothing I could do. I remember thinking to myself about how young I was and that I was about to meet God.

I am writing this book about hearing from God. However, I did not hear the voice of God as this happened. I slammed into the bridge, even though I was headed in what seemed to me to be another direction.

So where was God's voice in this? I believe that at the very moment I was headed towards that bridge, God put it in someone's heart to pray for me. I don't know who it was, but I believe that it was one of my parents, grandparents, uncles, aunts, friends or maybe just someone that I don't even know, praying for me in the spirit. I believe that because of the prayer of someone, God dispatched an angel. I believe I will see that angel and learn who prayed that prayer one day when I am in heaven.

That car was totaled out, and the only injury that I suffered was where a toggle switch put a small hole in my leg. I did not even go to the hospital.

A police officer came out and was writing up the report. I didn't know him, and he did not know me. He looked at me and asked if I was going to the hospital. I told him no, that I was fine. He told me that he was not going to write up a report because it would affect my driving record. Even then, despite my unwise choice, the favor of God was upon me and that accident did not report negatively on my driving record.

What I am about to share with you is more about me talking to God than it is about God talking to me. It is an account that some may find hard to believe but none the less it really did happen. I believe it is important for me to share this.

Several years ago, I was at a time in my life when I was preaching but not yet pastoring. I had preached out of town on a Sunday morning and then returned home. I went back that evening and preached again. I had returned home again after the evening service. Later that night, which was my normal routine for my business, I headed out in my big truck. I had to drive about 250 miles before I got to the first stop. Along the way, I managed to grab a quick nap in the truck. I then continued on my trip.

When I was young, I had a disorder that affected me by making me fall asleep within just a matter of minutes, or even seconds. I could be driving, working, or doing anything, when suddenly I would feel sleep coming on. I would get somewhere safe and fall fast asleep. In five minutes or so, I would wake and be fine. As I got older, this problem went away, thank the Lord! This could happen even if I had plenty of sleep but was worse if I had little, or not enough sleep. On this occasion, I had not had enough sleep.

I was in my truck driving in the North Georgia mountains when suddenly, I felt this sleepiness coming on. I knew I'd better get off the road but there was nowhere to pull over. I was very concerned, and I began to pray. My prayer went like this, "Now God, You know my situation. You know where I've been and what I have done. I am at a point now where I'm going to do all I know to do and trust you. In Jesus' name, I post angels around myself and this truck for protection. I claim the Blood of Jesus over myself and this truck. Father, I put it in your hands."

I was still looking for a place to pull over when I fell asleep. The truck's rocking woke me up, and the truck's right tires were off the road. The truck's left rear tires were in a slide headed down the mountain. I saw I was about to take out a sign. This was very concerning because it was obvious that the truck was about to roll down the mountain. Suddenly, the truck was picked up and set back into the road. Not even the sign was damaged! I started praising God with all that was within me! I believe God sent an angel because of that prayer and set that truck back right. I believe I will meet that angel one day. There is power in prayer! Praise God!

God doesn't just use angels when we have life or death situations!! I have a brother-in-law, named Charles Capelton. He is married to my sister, Margaret. Charles had a brother who we called Junior. Junior lived in Alabama, on the Warrior River. Junior was raised in an orphanage. He had a heart for orphans and had a big fish fry every year to raise money for them. A few years ago, Junior was planning to have his big fish fry to raise money for the orphans, but there was a problem. He had been sick and unable to do a lot of fishing. He simply did not know what to do. He did not have enough fish for the fish fry. Before I tell you the rest of this story, let me remind you of something that happened in the scriptures concerning Jesus and fish.

Jesus had gone to a deserted place by Himself but the multitudes soon followed Him. I recently heard a Bible teacher say that Bible scholars estimate that there may have been as many as 25,000 people there, including the women and children. He had compassion on them and healed their sick. We pick up this account in Matthew, Chapter 14, verse 15 through 17, ***"When it was evening, His disciples came to Him, saying, "This is a deserted place, and the hour is already late. Send the multitudes away, that they may go into the villages and buy themselves food. Jesus said to them, "They do not need to go away. You give them something to eat. And they said to Him, We have here only five loaves and two fish." He said, 'Bring them here to Me.' Then He commanded the multitudes to sit down on the grass. And He took the five loaves and the two fish, and looking up to heaven, He blessed and broke and gave the loaves to the disciples; and the disciples gave to the multitudes. So they all ate and were filled, and they took up twelve baskets full of the fragments that remained. Now those who had eaten were about five thousand men, besides women and children."***

Now Charles' brother, Junior, was at home, when a man came up to his house from the river. He told Junior that he had heard he could use some fish. Junior told him he sure could! The man then said he had fish to give to Junior and that they were in his boat. Junior told the man that he would walk down to the river with him and get the fish. The man said, "No, bring your truck down." Junior backed his truck to the water and that man had a lot of fish. They kept unloading fish. They loaded close to one thousand pounds of fish into Junior's truck! Junior pulled up the hill and started to clean

117

fish. He had been listening for the man's boat to start and it had not. Junior decided to go back down and say something else to the man. When he started down the hill, he noticed that the boat was gone. Junior told the neighbors what had happened, and no one remembered seeing the boat that he described or the man. Junior had his annual fish fry and raised money for the orphan children. There was not only enough fish for the event, but he even had fish left over! He believed, until the day he died, that God sent an angel with fish to him.

Isn't God wonderful? Psalms 91:11 says, *"For He shall give His angels charge over you, to keep you in all your ways."* I like the translation of this verse in The Message Bible. "*He ordered His angels to guard you wherever you go. If you stumble, they'll catch you; their job is to keep you from falling."* You see, there is no situation, whether large or small in your life, with which God is not concerned. All we must do is ask God for help. The Bible says in James 4:2, we have not because we ask not. The Bible also tells us that the angels only listen to the Word of God. Isn't it time that you start telling your angels to give you assistance in the name of Jesus?

# Chapter 12
## The Father's Love

I have a customer in Thomaston, Georgia, named Jinger Roberts. Jinger has a son named Hayden. She learned that God speaks in many different ways. He uses people, events, and circumstances, as a way of speaking into the lives of His children. Sometimes it is a major event that affects thousands, but at other times it is a comforting word for one person. In this case, it was for a twelve-year old boy named Hayden Roberts.

In December of 2012, Hayden made the decision to be saved by accepting Jesus Christ as his Lord and Savior. It was a time of great joy for his family, yet Hayden began to question many things. His main concern was that he did not want to go to hell when he died. After a few days of questions, Hayden spoke to his pastor again about his decision.

After speaking to his pastor, Hayden said, "He told me that he had never known a kid like me who wanted to know so much and have such a good understanding."

Hayden got baptized on December 9th, 2012. He was baptized early, and he and his family went home for Hayden to get cleaned up for the 11 o'clock service. It was then that he found the comfort he had been looking for.

As they turned into their driveway, a pair of yellow balloons were floating in the ditch and they were still filled with helium.

Upon closer inspection, they noticed there was a zip lock bag with a note attached to these balloons.

The note stated that the balloons were from Kirbyville, Texas. They had been let go by a children's discipleship class at Junction Baptist Church as part of a revival service on Saturday, December 8. Written on the note was John 3:16, ***"For God so loved the world that He gave His only begotten Son, that whosoever believeth in Him shall not perish, but have everlasting life."***

Hayden's mom, Jinger, said when she saw that verse she just lost it and started to weep. She said she knew it was a sign from God to let Hayden know that everything was just fine. God Speaks!

The Roberts family looked online and learned that Kirbyville, Texas, is a little over 700 miles from Thomaston, Georgia. The balloons traveled over four states in one night to make it to their house.

Jinger said that it amazed her that the balloons traveled so far and did not end up in a tree. It was also incredible that the balloons were barely deflated when they found them.

Jinger said, "I figure you can think deeply about this or you can take what you want from it. I just feel those balloons were confirmation from God for Hayden. It was no coincidence that those balloons would carry a note that referenced John 3:16, which talks about salvation."

Hayden agreed that finding the balloons and scripture made him feel better and eased his mind.

Jinger told Hayden, "This small thing could have landed anywhere. It may have touched someone, but it landed here, and it touched you!"

It is incredible that our father God loves us so much to speak into our lives in so many different ways. Don't put him into a box! He is God, and He knows how to speak! He has a great love for His children.

Our natural minds cannot fully comprehend the enormity, and the all-encompassing aspects of the love of God. In fact, the Bible says in Ephesians 3:17-19 that we cannot fully understand the depth, height, breadth, and length of God's all-powerful love. We must accept the fact that He loves us and cares for us. He is concerned about our welfare.

He cares if we eat or go hungry. He cares if we have a job or not. Our part is to walk in faith, love and trust our loving Father for the rest.

There was a widow in the Bible who needed food. God sent a prophet named Elijah to her. Elijah also needed food. Let's look at how she was not selfish but put her trust in God and in His prophet. In 1 Kings 17:10-16 we read the following account. *"So he arose and went to Zarephath. And when he came to the gate of the city, indeed a widow was there gathering sticks. And he called to her and said, "Please bring me a little water in a cup, that I may drink. And as she was going to get it, he called to her and said, "Please bring me a morsel of bread in your hand. So she said, "As the LORD your God lives, I do not have bread, only a handful of flour in a bin, and a little oil in a jar; and see, I am gathering a couple of sticks that I may go in and prepare it for myself and my son, that we may eat it, and die." And Elijah said to her, "Do not fear; go and do as you have said, but make me a small cake from it first, and bring it to me; and afterward make some for yourself and your son. For thus says the LORD God of Israel: 'The bin of flour shall not be used up, nor shall the jar of oil run dry, until the day the LORD sends rain on the earth.' So she went away and did according to the word of Elijah; and she and he and her household ate for many days. The bin of flour was not used up, nor did the jar of oil run dry, according to the word of the LORD which He spoke by Elijah."*

God is a need supplier to those who trust Him and believe Him by faith. He loves us greatly, and we can trust Him. Paul said in Philippians 4:19, *"And my God shall supply all your need according to His riches in glory by Christ Jesus."* I would like to share an account of a young man I know who used to go to church with me. He had a revelation that God is the supplier of all of our needs.

I was at Solid Rock Church, in the middle of a great Praise and Worship service. The Lord spoke into my spirit, told me to go, and give a word to this young man. At the time he was a youth pastor who was visiting from Georgia. He had brought his youth group with him. They had come about 300 miles. At first, I must confess, that I did not move. The Lord spoke the same thing into my spirit again and still I did not move. The Lord spoke the third time, and finally I walked over to the young man and I said, "God has given me a word for you." He looked at me and said that he wanted to hear it. "The word," I said, "is a scripture. It's Isaiah 40:31, *"But they that wait upon the Lord shall renew their strength; they shall mount up with wings as Eagles; they shall run, and not be weary; and they shall walk, and not faint."* He looked at me and said, "I receive that word Brother." At that point in time, he did not know how that word from the Lord would be repeated to him two more times.

He went back to Georgia with his youth group and was let go from his job. He had not been working at the church long. He had spent most of his money moving his wife and himself there from Alabama to take the position of youth pastor.

He was at home wondering what he would do when he received a phone call from a friend in Huntsville, Alabama. The man who called was his prayer partner. The youth pastor asked, "Did you hear what happened to me?" His friend said "No", but that he had a word for him from God. That was why he had called.

The youth pastor asked, "So, what is this word from God that you have for me?" His prayer partner replied, "They that wait upon the Lord shall renew their strength; they shall mount up with wings as eagles; they shall run and not be weary; and they shall walk, and not faint."

The Wednesday night service time came, and the youth pastor did not go because he was no longer employed with the church.

Soon after the church service had ended, there was a knock on his front door. It was a homeless man to whom the youth pastor had been ministering. The man said he went to church and noticed that he was not there. He said to the young man, "I've got two things for you." The youth pastor answered, "Okay, what have you got for me?" The homeless man said, "They that wait upon the Lord shall renew their strength; they shall mount up with wings as eagles; they shall run and not grow weary; and they shall walk and not faint." This was the third time that this word had come forth for this youth pastor. He knew God was up to something.

He asked the homeless man, "So what is the second thing you have for me?" The man handed him five dollars! The youth pastor told me that he hated to take the five dollars from this homeless person but that he really needed the money!

This young youth pastor was in a dilemma. He needed direction from God. He needed a job. He wanted to be in ministry, and he needed to put food on the table. Things had been going good at church so why was he without a job? It's one of those "What are You doing God?" moments!

I talked with the young youth pastor on the phone. He told me that someone had called and wanted him to interview for a job in radio. The young man had previously worked in the radio industry but had thought he did not want to get back into broadcasting. He told me the job was in Tuscaloosa, Alabama. I prayed for him over the phone, and God gave me a word of knowledge for him. The word that came into my spirit was "Northeast".

The word, "Northeast," did not seem to line up with the job offer, but I perceived in my spirit that I should ask a few questions. I asked him who was offering this job.

The young man told me the radio station was owned by Moody Radio. In fact, they had already contacted him about the job opening there. I said, "Brother, their center of operation is in Chicago, Illinois."

I got out a map and located Chicago on it. We compared it to where he was currently living in

Georgia, only to see that it was directly northeast of his current location!

It seemed as if he had his answer, but something didn't seem to fit at first. God had given me another word for him and the word was, "North". I told the young pastor what God had spoken and asked him for the address of the radio station located in Tuscaloosa, Alabama. I wondered if perhaps the radio station was located on North Street or something. He went and looked at the exact address of the radio station, and it was in a town that is beside Tuscaloosa, called Northport. God had given him ample direction through words of knowledge. The young man did go to work there. God blessed him and his family. He is a big sports fan, and one of his jobs was to head up the sports department. His favorite team is Alabama. He was able to get into the games and cover them not only for free but get paid to do it! God is wonderful!

On another occasion, I was talking to this brother over the phone. God showed me while we were praying that his family was about to get larger. A new baby was coming.

I must confess, I did not tell him right then. The next day I told my friend Kenny about it. Kenny said, "You had better call him and let him know." I said I would call him and I did, but a few days had passed.

When I called him, I told him I wanted to let him know of a word of knowledge God had given me while we were praying concerning his family expanding. He asked, "Have you heard the news? My wife is 5 weeks pregnant." I told him I had heard from God that a baby was coming, but I did not know it was so soon!  When God showed me, she was only about three weeks along.

I should have relayed the news then!  God had shown me, but I did not speak up at the right time. We live and learn, but it's best to flow with the Spirit while the Spirit of God is upon us to prophesy or to give a word of knowledge.  No matter what way God is using us we need to flow with His Spirit.

I believe God speaks to all of His children, but it's up to us to listen and discern.  Some will hear His voice but will convince themselves that it's not God.

I find that God speaks to me by speaking into my spirit and not my mind.  This may confuse some so I will explain.

We are a three part being.  We are spirit, soul, and body.  Some might think that the soul and spirit are the same, but the Bible teaches us that they are different.  God's Word shows us this in Hebrews Chapter 4:12, *"For the Word of God is quick, and powerful, and sharper than any two-edged sword, piercing even to the dividing asunder of soul and spirit, and of the joints and marrow, and is a discerner of the thoughts and intents of the heart.*

Additionally, we learn this from 1 Thessalonians 5:23, *"And the very God of peace sanctify you wholly; and I pray God your whole spirit and soul and body be preserved blameless unto the coming of our Lord Jesus Christ."*

The body is what we see when we look in the mirror.  The soul is our mind, will, and emotions. The spirit of man is what some would call our subconscious, or the heart.  It is that part of us that communicates with God.  The spirit is that part of us where we perceive what is right and wrong.

Our understanding of right and wrong is safest when it is filtered through the Word of God. People who have lived in the jungle and never heard the Word still have a perception of what is right and wrong.

As a born-again Christian, God speaks into our spirit.  We can know things by the Spirit of God.  As we follow His still, small voice, we will learn to trust our hearing and His direction.  Jesus told His disciples, before He was crucified, of the One that would come after His ascension from this earth and guide them.  Jesus said in John 16:13, *"Howbeit when He, the Spirit of truth, is come, He will guide you into all truth: for He shall not speak of himself; but whatsoever He shall hear, that shall He speak: and he will shew you things to come."*

In the Old Testament, the finger of God, which was the very Spirit of God, wrote His commandments on the tablets of stone.  However, we have a better covenant through the life, death, burial, and resurrection of His Son, Jesus Christ.  Jesus said the Holy Spirit would guide us into all truth.  The Holy Spirit lives inside of us, leading us and teaching us all things.  Look at John 14:17, *"The Spirit of truth, whom the world cannot receive, because it neither sees Him nor knows Him; but you know Him, for He dwells with you and will be in you."*  We know Him!!!  We can trust Him!!!  We can even remind God that we are trusting Him for His leadership through His Spirit because we have His Word on it.  As a believer, we are baptized into the faith by His Spirit.  No longer do we have to look at His commandments on stone tablets. Hebrews 10:16 tells us that the Spirit of God lives inside of us, and those commandments are written in our spirit on our heart. As we talked about earlier, God's love is wonderful and utterly amazing. When you get a revelation of walking in the divine love of God, those commandments that He has written in your heart are easy to keep. You will not want to steal or hurt someone when you walk in God's love. You will be able to keep those commandments because of His love flowing through you.

The soul is the part of us that we need to work on daily. It's in the realm of the soul that we are tempted and tried. Additionally, it is the part of us that talks and communicates with the people around us. It's where our thought life is.

My next point I can't totally back up with scripture. So please take it as my opinion and you may either agree or disagree.

I believe we were sent forth from God. We were sent forth from the Father Himself into our mother's womb. When we were there, I believe we were fully conscious of our surroundings. I believe we were almost totally functioning in the spirit realm. Even after birth, I believe babies are more aware of the spirit realm and not so much aware in the realm of the soul. As we grow, I believe we become more aware of the realm of the soul which is our mind, will, and emotions.

I believe that when we die and are in Christ, we will go back to being more in the spirit realm again. We will remember being sent forth from God and everything that has happened since. Let me say again that this is only my opinion.

Some may ask, "Will we remember all this that happened to us on earth after we die?" I think the answer is yes. When we die, we move to another location. I live in Haleyville, Alabama. If I move to Alaska, will I forget what I knew simply because I moved? I think not.

Does Jesus remember everything that has happened to Him? I think most of us would agree that He does. The scripture says that we will be like Him. That is found in 1 John 3:2, *"Beloved, now are we the sons of God, and it doth not yet appear what we shall be: but we know that, when He shall appear, we shall be like Him; for we shall see Him as He is."*

If we get to heaven and forget what happened down here, then what was the purpose of this life?

I believe we will remember and we will know that God is loving and a just God. I believe we will have the full revelation of how Satan is the author of sin, disease, destruction, and every evil work. Our loved ones who went to heaven before us because of disease, or the consequences of their sin, will openly share how their life was cut short because of issues the devil threw at them. We will see firsthand how God is a God of mercy, love, and appreciate that God is a God of justice. We will see and know how Jesus was made to be sin for us, and that He was the ultimate sacrifice for our sins. We will have full comprehension of how we were set free from the penalties of sin. We will totally walk in the righteousness of God through the blood of Jesus.

As I was writing this, I heard a minister make an interesting statement on his television program. He said, "Do you know that God loves you as much as He loves Jesus?" He gave his answer from John 17:23, *"I in them, and You in me; that they may be made perfect in one, You have sent Me, and have loved them as You have loved me."*

If we ever get a true revelation of the Father's love for us, I believe it will change our life. It will make us want to please Him more.

We please Him more when we tell others how much He loves them. We can do this by being a witness to others. We can talk about how good the Lord has been to us. We can brag on Jesus. We can give our own testimony. Sometimes, due to our lack of boldness, we are hesitant to ask individuals if they have made Jesus their Lord and Savior. We often don't realize that we can simply share with others our testimony of what the Lord has done in our own lives. Our testimony can become a seed in that person's life that God can use. We are called to be a witness for God, not the judge, jury, prosecutor, or defense attorney. We are just simply the witness. A witness only testifies about what they have seen and tells people about the great things that God has done in their life.

God loves us and wants to move on our behalf, but sometimes we have not because we ask not. We should listen to God's Spirit and see what miracles He will do and revelations He will show us.

When I was pastoring Bethel Baptist Church, there was a member there who was a registered nurse, named Debbie.

One night as the service was about to close in prayer, someone spoke up and said, "Let's pray for

Sister Debbie."

She had a lump in one of her breasts. She had been examined by more than one doctor, and the conclusion was that she needed to go to a bigger hospital and have a biopsy done. She was, in fact, going the next morning to have the procedure.

We gathered around Sister Debbie and anointed her with oil. We followed that up with the prayer of faith, in the name of Jesus.

The next day she was in Birmingham, Alabama, at the larger hospital, and the doctor could not find the lump at all. He could not biopsy what he could not find! Praise the Lord! God had healed her! We serve a loving God!

# Chapter 13
## Whom the Son Sets Free Is Free Indeed

Jesus was the master at hearing from God and being led by His Spirit. He walked here as a man. He was fully God, but He walked here as a man.

Being led of the Spirit, He was directed on multiple occasions to cast out devils. The Lord will use us in this area, as well, if we will follow His direction. We must know who we are in Christ.

In Mark, Chapter 5, Jesus had come into the country of the Gadarenes. He was met by a man that was possessed by demons. The man lived among the tombs. He had been bound often with shackles and chains, but he pulled the chains apart and broke the shackles.

When people saw this man, they just saw a lunatic. When Jesus looked at this man, He saw someone trapped by devils. Through the Holy Spirit, He knew the man's heart and knew he wanted to be free. That was why the man came and met Jesus.

Satan has no new ideas or devices. People cutting themselves and inflicting harm on themselves is a not a new idea. This man was doing that. He had so much pain on the inside that he was trying to match it on the outside. What a lie that came straight from the pit of hell!!! Don't you know it gave the demons pride to know they had that much control over the person?

Jesus commanded this legion of demons to come out of the man and they did. He cast them into a herd of swine. The swine, about two thousand of them, ran down a steep place and into the sea where they drowned.

A few years back, I was coming into the edge of Douglas, Georgia. If you remember, that is where my pastor friend Glenn Taylor lived. I called him on the phone, and he asked how far away I was. I said, about ten minutes. He wanted me to go and minister with him. I agreed to meet him and went over to his place.

Upon arrival, I asked him what was going on. We got into his van and started traveling to see a young man in his early twenties who had just gotten out of jail. He had been raped while in jail. His wife had left him. The judge had told him that if he went near her, he would give him 20 years in the state prison.

The young man's parents must have concluded that a phone call to the police would have just landed their son back in jail. If the ambulance were to be called, then the hospital wouldn't know what to do with him. They decided to call the preacher.

As we traveled on to where the young man was staying, Brother Glenn looked at me and said, "Let's pray in the Holy Ghost until we get there." That is just what we did.

We arrived where the young man was staying and went inside. The young man's father was there and said that the young man had not slept in three days. He was curled up in a fetal position on the floor. He looked totally defeated.

I was holding a bottle of anointing oil. Brother Glenn asked for the bottle and put some of the oil on his hands. He went over to the young man, reached down, and rubbed him on the back. He said, "Son, God loves you, and we love you too. Living a life without Jesus brings heartache and defeat."

Brother Glenn continued to witness to the young man. After a while, the young man agreed to pray the sinner's prayer.

When the young man started to talk, the demons began speaking out of him. They said they would not leave and tried to say a lot more. Brother Glenn shut them down in the name of Jesus. He commanded them to be mute in the name of Jesus.

As he tried to lead the young man in the sinner's prayer, the young man could not talk. Nothing came out of his mouth. Brother Glenn commanded the demons to loose the young man's tongue in the name of Jesus! They did, and Brother Glenn led him to Jesus. Praise God!

What happened next, I did not expect. The demons did not want to leave and were speaking all sorts of hateful things through the young man. Brother Glenn, being led by God's Spirit, addressed them one by one. Brother Glenn named a spirit and commanded it to leave. Then he named the next and commanded it to leave. He did this over and over. Suddenly, he looked at the young man and said, "You have been involved with a witch." The young man's father spoke up and confirmed it.

Brother Glenn raised the young man's shirt sleeve, and he had a devil tattoo on his arm. It was then that we learned he was a member of a satanic cult. He was a Satan worshipper.

Brother Glenn led him in a prayer denouncing all

relations with the devil, demons, witches, and so forth.

Brother Glenn continued casting out devils. Finally, he looked at me and asked me to get down close and help. He got more anointing oil and rubbed it on the young man. He said, "You foul demon of hurt, loose him in the name of Jesus!" The young man started to scream! Then a great peace came over him. He had been set free by the blood of Jesus!

After all the young man had experienced that evening, Brother Glenn suggested to the young man's father that he let him go and get some rest. He told him to let him sleep and to have the young man call him after he woke up.

That young man went forth, in time, to churches giving his testimony and leading many to Christ! Praise God!

We, as Christians, are to do the works of Jesus. The Bible says in Acts 10:38, *"God anointed Jesus of Nazareth with the Holy Spirit and with power, who went about doing good and healing all who were oppressed by the devil, for God was with Him."*

God intends for believers to walk in freedom. Many are not, "free indeed." Some are walking wounded from harsh words, death, divorce, abuse by parents, abuse by children, and the list goes on and on. What must one do to be free? How can anything good come from such pain?

God wants to set us free from that pain and heal our hearts. Freedom from pain can come as we allow God's healing power to work in our lives.

Galatians 5:1 says, *"Stand fast therefore in the*

*liberty by which Christ has made us free, and do not be entangled again with a yoke of bondage.*

Your purpose is more directly connected to your restoration than to your past. Your healing is more important than your wound.

We tend to magnify the trauma and tragedy, even after God has brought us out, more than we praise Him for His deliverance. However, we can't fully walk in the plans and purposes of God for our lives if all we want to do is talk about the past and live in the past. We must start talking about the God of today and what He wants to do now!

He wants you healed, and He wants to restore you. Then He can use you for a deeper, present purpose. Someone said, "God doesn't restore us to what we were but what He intended for us to be." If He has healed you or set you free from something, walk in that deliverance and glorify Him in your healing and move on. The Bible says, "We overcome by the Blood of the Lamb and the Word of our testimony." The devil may have attempted to destroy you with difficult situations throughout your life. God will use your victories to help someone else overcome that same situation in their life.

The devil will try to tell you that "no one understands your pain, your problems, or what you are going through." That is just not true. Jesus bore our pain, our sickness, and our hurts, so that we wouldn't have to bear them. Additionally, that is also having false pride, in thinking that no one has ever suffered or been hurt as badly as you have been.

We will fulfill the purpose God has for us when we leave the pain, past hurt, regrets, and every other distraction behind us. No matter what it takes we must move on. His purpose is ahead for us and not behind.

Leaving those hurtful times and wounds behind, while moving on, is sometimes the hardest thing you will ever do. It can't compare to what God has planned for you! When you understand that God wants to use the testimony of your deliverance from those types of situations to help others, it can help you shake off those nagging regrets and feelings of failure. His purpose is in your restoration. Walk in that purpose.

Romans 8:18 says, ***"For I consider that the sufferings of this present time are not worthy to be compared with the glory which shall be revealed in us."***

Some get mad at God and blame Him when things go wrong in life. They believe that God is responsible for their pain. Accidents, diseases, sickness, death, and disasters come as the result of the fall of man. Remember, John 10:10 says, ***"The thief does not come except to steal, kill and destroy but I (Jesus) have come that they might have life and that they may have it more abundantly!"***

God will take these things that happen in life and He will lead us through them. We can grow closer to Him during these things. It's up to us whether we receive His healing, or simmer in the pain and perhaps be destroyed. Adam knew no sickness before he knew sin and Satan.

Dr. John Alexander Dowie said, "Disease is the

foul offspring of its father, Satan, and its mother Sin."

Dr. Dowie was pastoring a Congregational church in a suburb of Sydney, Australia, in the 1870's. During this time a terrible plague swept through Western Australia. Multitudes of people died.

It is recorded in the book, "The Life of Alexander Dowie," written by Gordon Lindsay, that Dr. Dowie sat in his study, sobbing before God. He asked God these questions. "God, are you the author of sickness and disease? Did you send this terrible plague on this land? Are you going to destroy my whole congregation? Where did this plague come from? Who is the cause of it?"

Dr. Dowie had buried forty members of his congregation. Four more awaited burial, and he had just returned home from visiting more than thirty members, who were sick and dying.

"Then the words of the Holy Ghost inspired in Acts 10:38 stood out before me, all radiant with light, revealing Satan as the defiler, and Christ as the Healer," wrote this man of God.

Dr. Dowie said, "My tears were wiped away, My heart was strong. I saw the way of healing, and the door thereto, was opened wide, so I said, God help me now to preach the Word to all the dying around, and tell them how 'tis Satan still defiles, and Jesus still delivers, for He is just the same today." Within minutes, two men rushed into his study, pleading breathlessly, "Oh, come at once. Mary is dying!" Dr. Dowie ran down the street after them, not even pausing to take his hat. He was furious that Satan should have attacked this innocent young member of his flock. He found the girl in convulsions.

As Dr. Dowie entered Mary's room, her medical doctor, having given up on her, was preparing to leave. He turned to Dr. Dowie and remarked, "Sir, are not God's ways mysterious?"

The Word of God was burning in Dr. Dowie's heart. "God's way?" He thundered. "How dare you call that God's way? No sir, that is the devil's work!"

He challenged the physician, who was a member of his congregation, "Can you pray the prayer of faith that saves the sick?" The doctor replied, "You are much too excited sir, it's best to say God's will be done."

And he left. Isn't that strange? Many do not believe it is opposing God's will to be kept alive as long as possible by medicine, machines, and every other possible means. Yet, they believe that praying for healing to stay alive is working against God! And when they do die they call it God's will! If sickness is from God, then aren't you in sin by going to the doctor to get healed or get better? God is not the author of sickness and disease.

Still furious at Satan's attack, Dr. Dowie prayed the prayer of faith. The girl's convulsions ceased immediately. She fell into such a deep sleep that her mother and her nurse thought she had died. "She isn't dead," Dr. Dowie assured them. After several minutes, he awakened Mary. She turned to her mother and exclaimed, "Mother, I feel so well!"

Remembering how Jesus had ministered to the little girl He had raised from the dead in Scripture, Dr. Dowie asked, "Are you hungry?"

"Oh, yes," she agreed. "I'm so hungry."

He instructed the nurse to fix Mary a cup of hot chocolate, some bread and butter. Then he went into the next room, where her brother and sister lay sick with the same fever.

After prayer, they too instantly recovered. From that day on, Dr. Dowie ministered to his flock on divine healing and prayed for their healing. He never lost another member to the plague.

"As I went away from the home where Christ as the Healer had been victorious," Dr. Dowie wrote, "I could not but have somewhat in my heart of the triumphant song that rang through heaven, and yet I was not a little amazed at my own strange doings, and still more at my discovery that HE IS JUST THE SAME TODAY. And this is the story of how I came to preach the Gospel of Healing through Faith in Jesus."

# Chapter 14
## Children

Psalm 127:3-5 says, *"Behold, children are a heritage from the Lord, the fruit of the womb is a reward. Like arrows in the hand of a warrior, so are the children of one's youth. Happy is the man who has his quiver full of them."*

My quiver may not be full of children, but I do have two wonderful daughters that I love very much. I would like to share with you how our lives were blessed with our daughters, and how God moved mightily in making our family complete.

In 1996, after 13 years of marriage, we had no children and had been trying for a long time. Some good friends had successfully adopted a little girl from Romania. I was at the airport when he flew in with her. When he stepped off the jet, he handed her to me. Kaci was so sweet. She was almost three years old and was precious. After holding her for a few moments, I knew by the spirit that adopting a child from Romania was the route we should begin on our quest to have a child.

I contacted the same adoption service, and we were sent a photo of a little girl. From the moment we saw that little girl in the photo we knew we didn't need to look at any more pictures. She was the first child we looked at, and we decided she was the one for us. She was almost three when we started trying to get her out of the orphanage. In less than five months, we had her in our arms at home in Alabama.

Before the paperwork was finalized, something amazing happened. We had filed the appropriate paperwork and found out on a particular day that the Romanian Adoption Council had approved us to adopt Andrea.

This was exciting news, but the amazing thing was we also found out that same day that we were expecting a baby through the normal process of pregnancy. We both agreed that we would go forward with the adoption process. God knows how to work things out in His time.

When Andrea arrived in the United States on April 28th of 1996, she was 3 years and 4 months old. She weighed 18 pounds and was unable to speak either Romanian or English. The poor little girl had never been taught to talk. You see, she had been in an orphanage where there were too many children and not enough people to care for them properly. Most of her life had been spent in a crib.

Life in Alabama was a whole new world, so many things we take for granted were so strange to her. She was weak and could not stand for long. Andrea would look in bewilderment at the tv as if she had never seen one. I wondered if the orphanage even owned a television. She would rub the wall paper in amazement because it was strange to her.

Imagine our surprise when we went to feed her toddler food suitable for a three-year old. We learned she did not know how to eat real food. She would only take milk like an infant. Additionally, Andrea would only drink goat's milk, because that was what she was used to being fed while being raised in the orphanage in Romania. She refused every single bite of food.

We carried her to the doctor, and he put her on Pediasure mixed with milk. She refused a sippy cup if it had a lid but would drink from the cup if the top was not on it. Andrea would take the drink and hold it up to her mouth. She would not put it down until it was empty, even if she had to hold it for fifteen or twenty minutes. It would seem in the orphanage when the cup was put down it was gone. In time, I taught her that we had plenty.

I found a scripture and posted it in her room above her bed. It spoke of eating the good of the land.

I went to a revival meeting at Free Chapel in Gainesville, Georgia, pastored by Jentzen Franklin. The evangelist that night was R.W. Schambach. He prayed for Andrea's healing, in the name of Jesus. He also asked for a photo of her. He said he would be praying for her. Right after that she started drinking sweet tea. God heard that prayer.

Very shortly afterward, she took a bite of food while receiving occupational therapy at Children's Hospital, in Birmingham, Alabama.

An interesting God thing happened on the way to the hospital. As we were traveling, I saw almost a dozen solid green rainbows in the sky. They were not a bow shape but were straight. Their position in the sky was vertical. I watched them for approximately ten minutes.

This was a vision I was having while wide awake driving. This was seen only to me and no one else. What did it mean? Had someone died? I really did not know, but I perceived it was a sign from God.

I called and checked on family and friends.

Everyone was okay.  What did these green rainbows mean?  It was puzzling.

 At the time, I was pastoring Bethel Baptist Church, in Phil Campbell, Alabama.  I prayed for a week concerning the interpretation of this vision.  About a week later, as I was leaving church, I got my answer.  Suddenly, God started speaking in that still, small inward voice.  He asked, "What color were the rainbows son?"  I replied, "Green."  He said, "Green is for growth, and I am not finished with Andrea.  She will be okay!"  Praise God!  He gave me the gift of faith for Andrea with that Word!  I knew she would be okay.

 We had revival time coming up, and I had not yet asked anyone to be our guest minister.  I had one in mind and was prayerfully considering him.  I called a Pastor friend of mine named Tony and asked if he could run the revival.  He agreed to do so.  During the phone conversation, I shared with him the vision I had witnessed.  He said, "Brother Danny, did you know there is a green rainbow in the Bible?"  I said, "There is?"  He informed me it was found in Revelation 4:2-3, *"And immediately I was in the spirit: and, behold, a throne was set in heaven, and one sat on the throne.  And he that sat was to look upon like a jasper and a sardine stone: and there was a rainbow round about the throne, in sight like unto an emerald."*  Brother Tony asked me, "What color is an emerald?"  I said, "Emeralds are green!"  Praise God!

 I saw green rainbows in a vision, and John's revelation was a vision as well in which he saw the green rainbow around the Throne of God.  God was showing me something for Andrea!

That one sitting on the throne is God!  There were four living creatures around the throne saying, in verses 8-11, *"And the four beasts had each of them six wings about him; and they were full of eyes within: and they rest not day and night, saying, Holy, holy, holy, Lord God Almighty, which was, and is, and is to come.  And when those beasts give glory and honour and thanks to him that sat on the throne, who liveth for ever and ever, The four and twenty elders fall down before him that sat on the throne, and worship him that liveth for ever and ever, and cast their crowns before the throne, saying, Thou art worthy, O Lord, to receive glory and honour and power: for thou hast created all things, and for thy pleasure they are and were created."*

I was simply amazed that a green rainbow was in the Bible!  I just had not put the two together.

Andrea did learn to eat!  Praise God!  She went to school, and as a teenager, got her driver's license.  She has graduated from high school.  God is so wonderful.  She has a heart of worship!  She loves the Lord!  She is faithful to His house!  She loves His people!  Andrea is a great joy to all of our family and our church family as well!   Even though she is adopted, in my heart I consider her my real daughter.

Four months after Andrea arrived in the United States, my other daughter was born.  We named her Kristen.

I was in the delivery room when Kristen was born.  What a miracle of God that occurs when a baby comes into this world! I have had the privilege of watching Kristen grow to become a young lady. It seems like only yesterday that she was in her little dress, along with her sister, ready to go to church. Sometimes we would stop, eat breakfast along the way, and people would carry on about how pretty the girls looked!

Kristen loves to sing praises to God. She loved the Bible stories at church and at home as well. Kristen has loved the Lord since she was a little child. She has always enjoyed singing and playing gospel music!

Kristen has a heart for God and a heart for people. One summer, my girls, some friends and I, went to Six Flags Over Georgia. As we were leaving, we passed a homeless man. I put something in his hand. Kristen caught up to me and asked what that was all about. I explained that the man was apparently homeless. She said, "I'll be right back!" She ran back, grabbed her wallet, took some money out and gave to him generously! Kristen shows her love by doing for others. That is what Jesus taught us to do in His Word. I witnessed Kristen's love for God's creatures as she was a little girl. She would have had a zoo if it were up to her! God will use Kristen's love and faithfulness throughout her life, as she allows Him to guide her. She continues to use her talent in singing for the Lord.

I am a blessed father! Kristen and Andrea are beautiful young ladies with hearts of compassion. They are a joy to be around and a blessing from God!

Parents, I would like to encourage and exhort

you to always speak the Word of God over your children. You need to speak blessings over them and tell them of God's love and His amazing plan for their lives. I like to tell my children what it says in Jeremiah 29:11. It says, *"For I know the thoughts that I think toward you, says the Lord, thoughts of peace, and not of evil, to give you a future and a hope."* God has a special plan for your children, a specific calling and purpose for them. He knew them before they were in their mother's womb. They are not accidents, and they are beautifully and wonderfully made. There is nothing they can't accomplish with the Spirit of God living inside of them. The Word of God can change any situation in their life.

# Chapter 15
## Walking with God

We find a man in the Bible who learned to walk with God.  His name is Abraham.  He came from a people that worshipped many gods and did not know the one true God.

When we are introduced to him in scripture, his name is Abram.  God later changed his name to Abraham.

Abram heard the voice of God when he was in his home country and in his familiar surroundings.  He was living among the people he knew and to whom he was related.  This was his world, so to speak.

However, God spoke and gave him instructions. God speaks to us as well, through His Word and His Spirit.  Look at what God told Abram to do in Genesis 12:1-2, ***"Now the LORD had said unto Abram, Get thee out of thy country, and from thy kindred, and from thy father's house, unto a land that I will shew thee: And I will make of thee a great nation, and I will bless thee, and make thy name great; and thou shalt be a blessing:"***

God gave him an instruction, and Abram had a decision to make.  He  did not have to obey God. He could have chosen to stay in his comfort zone. That would have been the easy thing to do.  Thank God he did not!  You and I today are blessed because of Abraham obeying the voice of God many years ago.

Verse 3 of Genesis Chapter 12 says, ***"And I will bless them that bless thee, and curse him that curseth thee: and in thee shall all families of*** *the earth be blessed."*

The scripture says that all families of the earth shall be blessed because of Abram following God's voice.

How can that be? It is because through the line of Abraham came our Savior Jesus Christ. The sins of the whole world were put on Jesus at the cross. We must repent of our sins and make Jesus Lord to be assured of a home in heaven with God forever! Praise God!

Abram was 75 years old when he left his home town of Haran. We never get too old to hear and be blessed by obeying the voice of God. He left with his wife Sarai and his brother's son, Lot. Lot's father was dead.

It seemed as if Abram's life was a series of challenging circumstances. God would speak, and then He would give Abram direction. As Abram followed Him, he would face many difficult situations. These situations would require Abram to trust and rely totally on God. His faith in God's ability to perform His Word was often tested.

God appeared to Abram in verse 7 and said, *"To your descendants I will give this land."*

During an extreme famine in the land, Abram went into Egypt. He was in fear of his life because Sarai, his wife, was beautiful. He was afraid someone would kill him to get her.

You see, Sarai was not only his wife but was also his half-sister. He told her if anyone asked them she was to say that Abram was her brother. She ended up In Pharaoh's house. The Pharaoh wanted Sarai for his wife.

Pharaoh treated Abram well for her sake, but the

Lord plagued Pharaoh's house because of Sarai.

The Lord told the ruler in a dream that Sarai and Abram were married. Thankfully, the Pharaoh had not taken her as his wife. He confronted Abram, and Abram explained that he had been afraid for his life. The Pharaoh commanded his men concerning the safety of Abram and Sarai and told them to depart.

You see, Abram was a man who had his faults. He loved God, but he feared man. He had believed God enough to leave his own family and do what God had called him to do. Yet, he had so little faith that he was willing to let Pharaoh take his wife away because of fear. However, God used him anyway! There is hope for us all!!

God continued to bless Abram, and he became a very wealthy man in livestock, silver, and gold. Both he, and his nephew Lot, had large herds of livestock. This was another challenge in the life of Abram. He loved Lot, but there was much strife between his herdsmen and Lot's herdsmen.

Finally, Abram told Lot to go one way, and he would go the other. Lot looked at the well-watered plains of Sodom and decided to move there. It was a great place for livestock but not a great place to raise a family. Sodom was a place filled with sin.

God spoke to Abram again and told him that his seed would be like the dust of the earth. If a man could number the amount of dust of the earth, then his descendants could also be numbered.

Later, Abram heard that Sodom had been captured and all the inhabitants, including Lot and his family.

Abram armed three hundred and eighteen trained

servants who were born in his house and went and made war with the kings that had captured Sodom. God was with Abram and he prevailed.

After these things, Abram had a vision. God told Abram that He was Abram's shield. Abram expressed concern about being childless. God told him to look up into the heavens and count the stars if he could. God said this was how many descendants he would have.

God told Abram other things, including how his descendants would go into a land that was not theirs, and they would be slaves for 400 years.

Even after hearing all this from God, Abram became discouraged. His wife was old and had gotten impatient because they still had no children. Isn't that just like Satan? When you receive a Word from the Lord the devil immediately comes to steal it. He tries to discourage you from holding fast to what the Lord has promised you by His Word.

Sarai told him to sleep with their servant Hagar so Abram's seed could be preserved. He listened to her and soon after, Ishmael was conceived and then was born.

He jumped ahead of God. Abram made a mistake, but God was still with him and He blessed him. Some of Abram's mistakes caused him pain in time to come, and this particular mistake was no exception.

When Abram was 99 years old, the Lord appeared to him. God changed his name to Abraham, which means, "Father of many nations."

You see, God gave Abraham a word for his situation. He changed his name to a different word.  The word Abraham means, "Father of many nations".  The word Abram means, "Exalted Father or father of many".  By changing his name God made Abraham a promise.  We look at this in Genesis 17:15-17, *"And God said unto Abraham, As for Sarai thy wife, thou shalt not call her name Sarai, but Sarah shall her name be.  And I will bless her, and give thee a son also of her: yea, I will bless her, and she shall be a mother of nations; kings of people shall be of her. Then Abraham fell upon his face, and laughed, and said in his heart, shall a child be born unto him that is an hundred years old? and shall Sarah, that is ninety years old, bear?"*

The Lord told Abraham to name the child Isaac.  He said He would establish His covenant with him.

The Lord said that the child would be born on this set time next year.  That would make Sarah 90 years old.

The Lord appeared a second time to Abraham and had two angels with Him.  I believe one of these angels to be the pre-incarnate Christ.

Abraham had a calf killed, took butter and milk, and set it before them.  Sarah was nearby in a tent.  She heard their conversation.  Look at what the Lord said in Genesis 18:10-12.  *"And he said, I will certainly return unto thee according to the time of life; and, lo, Sarah thy wife shall have a son.  And Sarah heard it in the tent door, which was behind him.  Now Abraham and Sarah were old and well stricken in age; and it ceased to be with Sarah after the manner of women. Therefore, Sarah laughed within herself, saying, After I am waxed old shall I have pleasure, my lord being old also?"*

Yes, Sarah laughed. However, can you imagine getting news at 89 years of age that you are going to have a baby at age 90? Sarah denied laughing.

Afterward, the men rose and looked toward Sodom. At this point, Abraham could have gone back into the tent and had an exciting conversation with Sarah about the news! After all, they had waited many years for a child. Instead, Abraham chose to walk with God. As he walked with God, he learned of the plan to destroy Sodom. It pays to walk with God and to be tuned into His voice! We can learn things we otherwise would not know by spending time with Him. When we spend time with Him and wait on Him, God will show us things!

Sarah gave birth to Isaac just as the Lord had told her. He is never slack concerning His promises.

Despite the great joy of having little Isaac in the camp, a situation arose with the presence of Ishmael and his mother Hagar living there. It so happened that one day Ishmael laughed at Isaac. Sarah decided that he and his mother had to go. Poor Abraham! Imagine having to choose between his two sons. Abraham loved Ishmael. This was one of the pains of his sin. However, God had made a promise to Abraham, even for Ishmael. Out of his seed would come a nation. The mother and son were told to go. God remembered His promise to Abraham for Ishmael. He delivered him and his mother from near death in the wilderness, supplying them with food and water.

When Isaac was a young man, or even a teenager, God once again would see whether

Abraham truly trusted Him. He had gone through many challenges to see exactly where his level of faith and commitment in God was. This time, it was as if God were saying, "Abraham, I want more than the land of your birth. I want more than Lot. I want more than Ishmael. I want Isaac. I want more than your best. I want your all."

Jesus wants more than our best. He wants our all. He can do more with your worst than you can do with your best.

He told him to go and offer Isaac up as a burnt sacrifice on a mountain in Moriah.

Genesis 22:4 says, ***"Then on the third day Abraham lifted up his eyes and saw the place afar off."***

Notice that in this verse he saw the place. There is no doubt that Abraham had a heavy heart. We have already established that he was human. He made mistakes. He hurt just like others would hurt.

Abraham put the wood on Isaac's back. It was in that same area, and perhaps that same hill, that God ordained for His Son Jesus to have wood placed on His back. He was going up a hill carrying a cross to lay down His life as a sacrifice for the sins of the world. Jesus was the Lamb of God that came to take away the sins of the world.

Abraham told his servants, "I will go yonder with the lad and worship, and 'we' will come back to you." Abraham knew that God would make everything alright. He just had to trust Him.

It must have been hard when Isaac asked his father about where was the animal that was to be sacrificed. Can you imagine how hard it was when Abraham had to tie up his son and took the knife in

154

his hand to kill him?

Notice what happened in Genesis 22:11-12, *"**And the angel of the LORD called unto him out of heaven, and said, Abraham, Abraham: and he said, here am I. And he said, lay not thine hand upon the lad, neither do thou anything unto him: for now I know that thou fearest God, seeing thou hast not withheld thy son, thine only son from Me.**"*

Notice in the next verse that Abraham saw the place again that God had told him to take Isaac and sacrifice him. Now it was from a different perspective.

Genesis 22:13 says, *"**And Abraham lifted up his eyes, and looked, and behold behind him a ram caught in a thicket by his horns: and Abraham went and took the ram, and offered him up for a burnt offering in the stead of his son.**"*

When we hear the voice of God, we might be asked to do something that seems hard or almost impossible. Yet, do we trust Him? Perhaps what God tells us doesn't line up with our plans or doesn't look like we thought it would or should.

Abraham listened and followed God as God spoke to him. It was not easy, but God blessed him for his obedience!

What Abraham could not see was that while he was going up one side of that mountain with Isaac, the Lord was leading a ram up the other side! God is our provider, He is Jehovah Jireh!!!

GOD SEES BOTH SIDES OF THE MOUNTAIN! We can trust Him! We have seen over and over that He speaks, but He wants you and I to know that we can trust Him.

Abraham learned that there are three things we must do when we are in between the two mountains: When we can't explain it; When we don't understand it; When we don't even like it we need to:

1. Walk on
2. Worship On
3. Wait On

I like Isaiah 40:31, *"But they that wait upon the Lord shall renew their strength; they shall mount up with wings as eagles; they shall run, and not be weary; and they shall walk, and not faint."*

# Chapter 16
## In My Father's House


Jesus said in John 14:1-3, *"Let not your heart be troubled: ye believe in God, believe also in me. In my Father's house are many mansions: if it were not so, I would have told you. I go to prepare a place for you. And if I go and prepare a place for you, I will come again, and receive you unto myself; that where I am, there ye may be also."*

Jesus knew that it is appointed unto man once to die. He talked about His Father's house. Heaven is a great and unimaginable place.

I am thankful to have been raised by a father and mother who taught me about our Father in heaven's house.

I started off in chapter one telling you about my sister, Margaret and how that she was a miracle baby. I shared the account of how she was not supposed to live. If you remember, I also told of how she was not supposed to be able to have a child. However, then her son Branden was born.

An earthquake, so to speak, came into our lives on August 21, 2012. Branden was on the job when his heart stopped beating. He was taken to the hospital. However, despite everything the doctors could do, Branden died. He left behind a wife, a five-year old son named Noah, a two-year old son named Konner, and a baby on the way. That baby was born January 18th, 2013. Branlee is her name.

It does not seem fair. Branden was a hard-working young man and was loved greatly by our family. However, we know that tragedy, sin, sickness, and death came into the world because of the devil. The fact is, he is the god of this world according to 2 Corinthians 4, verse.4. When Adam sinned, he gave the devil control over this world. We can blame the unfairness of life on Satan and sin.

There are things in this life that will not fully make sense until we get to heaven. Surely, we now see through a glass darkly, but one day we will see Jesus face to face. These heartaches will be behind us, and they won't seem to matter anymore.

Have you ever turned your head for a moment in a store, and your little child has disappeared from your sight? For fifteen seconds, they are out of sight and then you find them. It seems like forever. Once I was with a friend, and she lost sight of her granddaughter for about five minutes.

That is a bad feeling. The sudden loss of someone we love and treasure is so hard, even if it is temporary. Nothing seemed to matter until we found her granddaughter. Funny how the minute we found her granddaughter the gut wrenching feeling of uncertainty and loss was suddenly swept away. It was replaced with joy and thankfulness of being reunited.

That's the way it will be when we are reunited with our loved ones who have gone on to their heavenly home. When we are with them, the time apart won't matter anymore. My brother Phillip says, concerning our nephew Branden, "We will be right behind him." It's true that life is short. Even if we live one hundred years, it's still short.

I believe my sister Margaret loved Branden as much as any mother could possibly love their child. However, her faith in God has sustained her. He was his father Charles' only son. Charles loved Branden greatly and with a father's heart. A reunion is coming in heaven one day.

Margaret asked me to conduct Branden's funeral. I told her that I would. The next morning while in the shower, I was praying. I heard the still, small voice of God prompting me to ask my brother Phillip to speak at the funeral. Phillip has not had much experience with speaking in front of crowds, so I did not know how he would react to my asking him. However, I knew I had heard God's voice.

I was picking Phillip up that morning at his home to take him to Jasper, Alabama, to get his vehicle, which had been in the shop for repairs. I pulled into his driveway, and he got in my car with a note in his hand. He told me he had something for me. I stopped him and said, "I am sorry for interrupting you, but I must ask you something. Will you speak at Branden's funeral?" He graciously agreed. His note, of course, had thoughts and scriptures on it. They fell right into place with the sermon God had given me. The presence of God was evident and powerful at Branden's funeral.

My friend, whose granddaughter had inadvertently wandered off in the store, lost her daughter, the child's mother in a tragic car accident. It was a time of great sadness for her and the whole family.

I could go on and on about those I have known that have gone on to be with the Lord. They surely know, without any doubt, that God speaks because they are in His presence in heaven. They get to hear His sweet voice as they are there with Him and seeing Him face to face!!

The Bible tells us how much Job suffered. Satan had been searching the earth and had decided he wanted to come against Job. He came and destroyed his life. Satan was hoping that Job would curse God and turn his back on God. Job was a man who operated in the blessings of God and had much influence in the land during his life. We read that Job was constantly telling his friends and neighbors of God's goodness and mercy. Satan came to destroy that relationship between Job and His God. Job lost everything including his friends, family, and his great wealth. In fact, Job was accusing God of being the one that was responsible for the tragedy he had suffered. He even wanted to argue with God. Then God spoke! Afterward, Job saw himself as dependent totally upon God. Job had gone to the ash heap looking for God. Why the ashes? That was where he had offered up burnt offerings unto the Lord. That is where he went to worship God. That had been a communication place between him and God.

Are you having trouble hearing from God, but you are a Christian? Go back to where you heard Him last. God is still there waiting. That communication will be restored, because God did not move. He wants to communicate His love and His guidance to you. Remember though, the primary way He speaks to us is through His Word. Read it, gain revelation, and insight.

Often, when God does speak in that still small,

sweet voice, it will be by His Holy Spirit bringing back to our remembrance a specific scripture.

# Chapter 17
## God's Word Works

Hopefully by now, I have encouraged, exhorted, and shown you scripturally, that God wants to speak to you on a daily basis. You see, we were always supposed to have that close relationship from the very beginning when God created Adam and Eve. In Genesis, it says that God walked and talked with Adam and Eve in the cool of the evening. Even after they had sinned and disobeyed, God called out to them. He was ready to spend another evening with them, fellowshipping in the beautiful garden He had created for them. Satan messed it all up. Then Jesus came and restored that relationship with our Heavenly Father through His death, burial, and resurrection.

We as Christians need to have an understanding of the power of God's Word. One scripture can change your circumstances. Having a Bible in one's possession is not enough. Knowing the contents of that Word in one's memory is not enough. We must believe and proclaim the Word over our circumstances. The most important scripture in God's Word is the one we need to stand on at that moment. The genealogies in scriptures are important. However, if a person does not know Jesus as their Savior, a more relevant scripture is John 3:16. *"For God so loved the world, that He gave only His begotten Son, that whoever believes in Him should not perish but have everlasting life."*

Let's look at some life changing scriptures.

When you became a born-again believer, the third person of the Godhead came to live in you. John 14:17 says, "You know Him". Let's look at that verse, **"...the Spirit of truth, whom the world cannot receive, because it neither sees Him nor knows Him; but you know Him, for He dwells with you and will be in you."** As a believer, the Spirit of God is in you.

Notice in that verse Jesus said, "You know Him." You have Jesus' Word, as a born-again, Spirit filled believer, that you know God's Spirit. We don't have to live our lives in doubt, always wondering what to do, or how to go forward. We can look in the mirror and remind ourselves that we know God's Spirit. We can speak and say, "Holy Spirit, I know you! You are in me. I'm not living a life that is without guidance! I hear your still, small voice. You are my best friend!"

Leigh Ann Soesbee is over Prayer and Healing school at Rhema Bible Training College, in Broken Arrow, Oklahoma. She tells the story of a woman who came to the healing center with cancer. The healing technicians had been working with her. They had brought her to Mrs. Leigh Ann for advice. Mrs. Leigh Ann told her to find one scripture. The woman was to quote it and stand on it. She asked the woman which scripture resonated with her in the Word.

She liked 2 Corinthians 2:14, **"Now thanks be to God who always leads us in triumph in Christ."** The woman told Mrs. Leigh Ann, "I'm not a preacher." Mrs. Leigh Ann reminded her that she was a believer. As a believer, we all have a legal, covenant right to claim God's promises and stand on God's written Word.  Jesus purchased that right for us with His blood on the cross.

The woman with the cancer started saying in a timid voice, "I always triumph in Christ, I always win."  Mrs. Leigh Ann told her to say that verse several times over the weekend.

On Monday morning, the woman came back to the prayer and healing center.  She was there waiting on Mrs. Leigh Ann to arrive. When she got there, the woman exclaimed with a passionate tone in her voice, "I always triumph in Christ!  I always win!"

She told Mrs. Leigh Ann that she was healed of cancer.  She explained that she had quoted that scripture on the hour, every hour, over the entire weekend!

She went back to her cancer doctor, and he confirmed that she was cancer free!  Praise God! We can stand on His Word!  In life's difficult situations, we can remind ourselves that Paul said in 1 Corinthians. 2:16, *".....We have the mind of Christ."*

Another promise we as believers can stand on is in 1 John 2:20. *"But you have an anointing from the Holy One, and you know all things."*

Do we know all things with our natural mind?  No, but the Holy Spirit of God lives in us, and He knows all things!  He will reveal to us all that we need to know as we seek Him.  He is our helper.

How can we remain mentally perplexed when He is our helper?  He will always guide us into truth.

One way He guides us is when we pray in the spirit and then interpret the prayer.   1 Corinthians

164

14:15 states, *"I will pray with the Spirit, and I will also pray with the understanding. And I will sing with the Spirit, and I will sing with the understanding."* This verse is referring to praying in the spirit and then allowing God's Spirit to lead us in the interpretation of that prayer. We first pray things out in the spirit and then the understanding comes.

He helps us when we are weak. Romans 8:26 says, *"Likewise the Spirit also helps in our weaknesses. For we do not know what we should pray for as we ought, but the Spirit Himself makes intercession for us with groanings, which cannot be uttered."*

We can be in a situation where we do not even know how to pray. I can tell you there have been times when I have felt so overwhelmed, I could not pray, or find the words to express what that pressing need was in prayer. Praise God! That is when His Spirit helps us!

When we need building up, pray in the spirit. Jude 20 says, *"But you, beloved, building yourselves up on your most holy faith, praying in the Holy Spirit."*

We can obtain victory over depression by praying in the spirit. Many victories belong to us through the Word and prayer.

Are you battling fear? 2 Timothy 1:7 says, *"For God has not given us a spirit of fear, but of power and of love and of a sound mind."*

God has not given us fear, or depression either. What has He given us? Power, love, and a sound mind! Claim it Christian friend! Don't let the enemy win.

Some people can get weighted down with the burdens of life. They carry their own concerns and perhaps the burdens of others as well. Their intentions may be good, but it's a load we are not designed to carry. It can break one down physically, as well as emotionally.

I heard a story of a pastor who was dying of old age but was only 39 years old. A seasoned minister asked him if he was having trouble eating and sleeping. He said that he was because he constantly worried about his congregation.

The minister informed him that he was in sin. He was not called to carry that load. He told the pastor what the Word says in 1 Peter 5:7, *"Casting all your care upon Him, for He cares for you."*

He told him that we are to do our part. Then we are to rest in God. He can handle it. We must trust Him.

That pastor followed the advice and went on to retire at age 75. He let it be known, however, that he was not retiring from preaching. He would be glad to fill the pulpit when needed.

There is no area of your life that God is not concerned about. If it concerns you, He has the answer!!! If we have any kind of need, we can stand on, quote, and believe God's Word.

Philippians 4:19 tells us, *"And my God shall supply all your needs according to His riches in glory by Christ Jesus."*

Whatever your need is, stand on that verse. Then just begin to thank God for His provision! The prayer of faith requires that we ask God and then believe that we receive.

Mark 11:22-24 says, *"So Jesus answered and said to them, "Have faith in God. For assuredly, I say to you, whoever says to this mountain, 'Be removed and be cast into the sea,' and does not doubt in his heart, but believes that those things he says will be done, he will have whatever he says. Therefore, I say to you, whatever things you ask when you pray, believe that you receive them, and you will have them."*

It is the will of God for us to pray this way according to this verse. This is the prayer of faith. Notice that Jesus tells us to speak to the mountains in our lives.

A lot of Christians don't realize there are different types of prayer. They will say, "God's will be done." However, His Word is His will.

The time to pray that kind of prayer is when we pray the prayer of consecration, or dedication, of our life to God and His purposes. Jesus did this at the garden of Gethsemane. He did not want to be crucified. However, He said, "Not my will, but your will be done."

He knew when he prayed for the sick that it was God's will to heal them. Look at Isaiah 53:5. *"But He was wounded for our transgressions, He was bruised for our iniquities; The chastisement for our peace was upon Him, And by His stripes we are healed."*

Why would Jesus doubt the will of the Father when He already had God's Word on it?

God is kind and loving. He heals, forgives, is merciful, and even gives us strength at any age!

Ps 103:3-5 says, *"Who forgives all your*

*iniquities, Who heals all your diseases, Who redeems your life from destruction, Who crowns you with lovingkindness and tender mercies, Who satisfies your mouth with good things, So that your youth is renewed like the eagle's."*

Praise God! He is so wonderful!

We do not have to be anxious. We can come to our father God and remind Him that we are His child. We can tell Him that we love Him. Just keep standing on God's Word.

If you are not sure of the direction to take on a certain situation, just praise God for His provision. The answer will come with peace from God. Follow peace. That velvety feeling in your spirit, that's God. Philippians 4:6-7 says, ***"Be anxious for nothing, but in everything by prayer and supplication, with thanksgiving, let your requests be made known to God; and the peace of God, which surpasses all understanding, will guard your hearts and minds through Christ Jesus."***

Finally, remember this promise. Philippians 4:13 says, ***"I can do all things through Christ who strengthens me."***

Praise God! If you will start speaking what God's Word says over the situations in your life, you will start seeing things change. I once heard a minister say, if you are at home, sitting in your chair, and you are looking for your dog, you don't start saying, "Here Kitty, Kitty!" The dog will not come, but your cat might show up. Some of you have been wanting the dog to come but are calling the cat. You are speaking doubt and unbelief over your life, and then wondering why things aren't working the way they should! God's Word works, but you must speak it out over your life on a continual basis!!

I have shared just a small sampling of the many promises in God's Word! I hope, and pray, that these promises will encourage you. I hope that you will grab hold of these promises, stand on them, and believe God for whatever you need in your life. God's Word works!!!

In closing, I want to thank God for allowing me to be born into a Godly Christian home. I'm thankful for my Christian parents. I'm thankful for a Christian brother, sister, and their families. I am thankful for my daughters, Andrea, and Kristen. I am thankful for the many Godly friends, God ordained relationships, and how God has used these wonderful people to speak into my life.

I am thankful for Pastor Benny Knight and Solid Rock Church. Most of all, I am thankful for my Lord and Savior, Jesus Christ.

Dear Friend, do you know where you would spend eternity if your life ended today? Are you sure that you have asked Jesus to come into your life? Do you feel like you are far away from God yet at one time accepted what Jesus did on the Cross? If the answer is yes to any of those questions, we would like you to repeat this simple prayer with us. Father God, I come before You and repent of my sins. I ask You to forgive me, cleanse me and come live inside of me. I believe that your Son, Jesus Christ, died on the cross so that I wouldn't have to pay for my sins. Glory to God!! Jesus now lives inside of you, and one day you will spend eternity with Him in heaven. If you prayed that prayer, we encourage you to get in a good bible believing church. Going to a local church can strengthen you in your daily walk with the Lord. A local church can be a vital source of support and help in those tough times that we all face. We also suggest that you read your Bible every day, and spend time with your Father God, who loves you.

# Power Scriptures

We believe the Bible is the living Word of God, and in it are scriptures that apply to every problem or situation we face. We also believe that we must speak to situations in our life and speak the Word of God in those situations. Perhaps you are needing healing or need peace? We have listed below a few scriptures that will encourage you and help your faith to grow.

### There is Nothing Impossible with God:
**Mark 11:22-24** – So Jesus answered and said to them, "Have faith in God. For assuredly, I say to you, whoever says to this mountain, 'Be removed and be cast into the sea,' and does not doubt in his heart, but believes that those things he says will be done, he will have whatever he says. Therefore, I say to you, whatever things you ask when you pray, believe that you receive them, and you will have them.

**Mark 10:27** - But Jesus looked at them and said, "With men *it is* impossible, but not with God; for with God all things are possible."

### We Are Victorious Through Jesus:
**2 Corinthians 2:14** - Now thanks *be* to God who always leads us in triumph in Christ, and through us diffuses the fragrance of His knowledge in every place.

**Romans 8:37** - Yet in all these things we are more than conquerors through Him who loved us.

**Walking in Wisdom and Knowledge:**

**1 Corinthians 2:16 -** For who has known the mind of the Lord that he may instruct Him? But we have the mind of Christ.

**1 John 2: 20 –** But you have an anointing from the Holy One, and you know all things.

**John 14:16-17 -** And I will pray the Father, and He will give you another Helper, that He may abide with you forever—the Spirit of truth, whom the world cannot receive, because it neither sees Him nor knows Him; but you know Him, for He dwells with you and will be in you.

**When you Need Peace:**

**2 Timothy 1:7 -** For God has not given us a spirit of fear, but of power and of love and of a sound mind.

**Psalm 4:8 -** I will both lie down in **peace**, and sleep; For You alone, O Lord, make me dwell in safety.

**John 14:27 -** Peace I leave with you, My peace I give to you; not as the world gives do I give to you. Let not your heart be troubled, neither let it be afraid.

**When You Have Financial Needs:**

**Philippians 4:19 -** And my God shall supply all your need according to His riches in glory by Christ Jesus.

**Psalms 37:25 -** I have been young, and *now* am old; Yet I have not seen the righteous forsaken, Nor his descendants begging bread.

### Why Being Filled With God's Spirit is Important:

**1 Corinthians 14:15 -** What is the conclusion then? I will pray with the spirit, and I will also pray with the understanding. I will sing with the spirit, and I will also sing with the understanding.

**Romans 8:26 -** Likewise the Spirit also helps in our weaknesses. For we do not know what we should pray for as we ought, but the Spirit Himself makes intercession for us with groanings which cannot be uttered.

**Jude 20: -** But you, beloved, building yourselves up on your most holy faith, praying in the Holy Spirit.

### When You are Feeling Anxious and Worried:

**1 Peter 5: 7 –** Casting all your care upon Him, for He cares for you.

**Philippians 4:6-7 –** Be anxious for nothing, but in everything by prayer and supplication, with thanksgiving, let your requests be made known to God; and the peace of God, which surpasses all understanding, will guard your hearts and minds through Christ Jesus.

### God Is Our Healer:

**Isaiah 53:5 –** But he was wounded for our transgressions, He was bruised for our iniquities; The chastisement of our peace was upon Him, And by His stripes we are healed.

**Ps 103: 3-5 –** Who forgives all your iniquities, Who heals all your diseases, Who redeems your life from destruction, Who crowns you with lovingkindness and tender mercies, Who satisfies your mouth with good things.  So that your youth is renewed like the eagle's.

**God Empowers Us to Live:**
**Philippians 4:13** – I can do all things through Christ who strengthens me.
**Romans 8:11** - But if the Spirit of Him who raised Jesus from the dead dwells in you, He who raised Christ from the dead will also give life to your mortal bodies through His Spirit who dwells in you.

Made in the USA
Lexington, KY
18 December 2018